The Gracious Flow of Dharma

Acharya S. N. Goenka

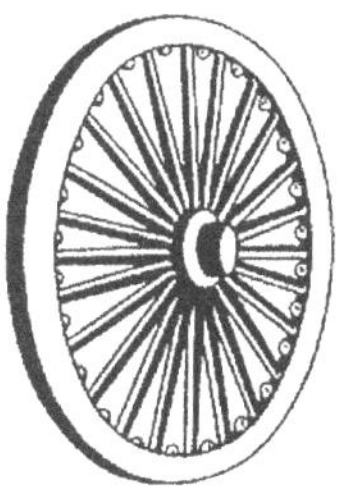

Vipassana Research Institute
Dhammagiri, Igatpuri 422403

The Gracious Flow of Dharma

First Edition : November 1994
Reprint : 1996, 1997, 2002, 2006, 2010, 2013, June 2017

E08

ISBN: 978-81-7414-015-9

Published by:
Vipassana Research Institute
Dhamma Giri, Igatpuri 422 403
Dist. Nashik, Maharashtra, India
Tel: [91] (2553) 244998, 244076,
244086, 244144, 244440
Email: vri_admin@vridhamma.org
Website: www.vridhamma.org

The Gracious Flow of Dharma

Contents

Preface

Preface

Vipassana Research Publications is pleased to offer this book of Mr. S. N. Goenka's public talks.

Mr. Goenka left his homeland of Myanmar (Burma) in 1969, to come to India, the land of his ancestors, to teach Vipassana meditation. Vipassana originated in India but was lost to the country. Fortunately it was preserved in its pure form for over two millenia in the neighbouring country.

In the twenty-four years since he left Myanmar, Mr. Goenka has introduced Vipassana to tens of thousands of people worldwide. His primary focus has always been on the practical aspect of the technique. He has conducted nearly 400 ten-day Vipassana courses in India and a dozen other countries, and many thousands of people have learned Vipassana in courses conducted by his assistant teachers.

In addition to his teaching work, Mr. Goenka has presented Vipassana to the general public through hundreds of public discourses in different countries, and in different cities in India. Mr. Goenka has given the majority of these talks in Hindi; the remainder, as in the present volume, in English. Initially, these talks were given in one session. In recent years, however, Goenkaji has developed an additional format of speaking for a series of three or five consecutive evenings, in order to treat the subject in greater depth.

The three-day series of public talks contained in this book was given in Hyderabad, A.P., India from July 22 to 24, 1993. For publication purposes, it has been titled "The Gracious Flow of Dharma."

The Sanskrit word *Dharma* (which is spelled *Dhamma* in the Pāli language) originally meant "the law of nature" or "the truth." In today's India, unfortunately, the word has lost its original meaning, and is mistakenly used to refer to "sect" or "sectarianism." Using this theme as an introduction, Goenkaji explains that Vipassana meditation teaches how to live a life of pure Dharma—a life full of peace, harmony and goodwill for others. This subject is particularly relevant in India today—and indeed the whole world—where sectarianism and communalism have divided large sections of society and caused acute suffering.

May these talks give inspiration to all to walk on the path of pure Dharma and gain the lasting benefit of real peace and happiness.

Vipassana Research Institute

July 1994

Dharma na Hindū Bauddha hai,
Sikkha na Muslima Jaina.
Dharma citta ki śhuddhatā,
Dharma śhānti sukha chaina.

Dharma is not Hindu nor Buddhist,
not Sikh, Muslim, nor Jain;
Dharma is purity of heart,
peace, happiness, serenity.

—Hindi doha of S. N. Goenka

Day One:
Dharma and Sectarianism

Friends, seekers of peace and harmony:

Everyone seeks peace. Everyone seeks harmony. Life is full of misery, misery of one kind or another, due to this reason or that reason. There is misery everywhere. How can we come out of misery? How can we live peaceful, harmonious lives, good for ourselves and good for others?

The sages, saints and seers of India—the wise, enlightened ones—asked: "Why is there misery?" and "Is there a way out of misery?" There are innumerable apparent reasons why there is misery. But we cannot come out of misery by eradicating these apparent reasons. The real cause of misery lies deep within ourselves. And unless this deep-rooted cause of misery is eradicated, we can never experience real peace, real harmony or real happiness.

How can we eradicate the deep-rooted cause of misery within ourselves? Everyone who was wise and enlightened realized that the only way to eradicate misery was by following the path of Dharma. If one lives the life of Dharma, one is definitely coming out of misery. Dharma and misery cannot co-exist. But the difficulty came when, after a few centuries, people forgot what Dharma was. When one does not understand the real meaning of Dharma, how can one apply Dharma in life?

Two thousand years ago in India, there were two distinct traditions. One tradition gave importance to the purity of Dharma. The other gave importance to sectarian rites, rituals, religious ceremonies, external appearances, and so on. In those days the tradition of pure Dharma was quite strong, but slowly it became weaker and weaker, and eventually vanished from India. What was left had no trace of pure Dharma. It is very unfortunate that we have lost Dharma. When one speaks of Dharma in today's India, the question that arises in the audience's mind is: "Which Dharma? Hindu-dharma, Buddhist-dharma, Jain-dharma, Christian-dharma, Muslim-dharma, Sikh-dharma, Parsi-dharma, or Jewish-dharma? Which Dharma?"

It is a great pity that we have totally forgotten pure Dharma. How can Dharma be Hindu, Muslim, Christian, Jain, Parsi, or Sikh? This is impossible. If Dharma is pure Dharma, it is universal. It cannot be sectarian. Sectarian rites and rituals differ from one sect to another. The so-called "Hindu-dharma" has its own rites, rituals and religious ceromonies; its own beliefs, dogmas, and philosophies; and its own external appearances, and disciplines, such as fasting. It is the same with the Muslim-dharma, Christian-dharma, Sikh-dharma, and so on. But Dharma has nothing to do with all these. Sectarianism is divisive. Dharma is universal: it unites.

The meaning of Dharma in the ancient language of India has been lost. Unfortunately, our country has lost the bulk of its ancient literature and scriptures. This literature was preserved and is still being maintained in the neighbouring countries. When we study these writings it becomes so clear what the people of this country meant by Dharma in ancient times. The definition was *"Dhāretī ti dharma"*—what one holds, what one contains, is Dharma. This means what one's mind is holding, what one's mind is containing, at this moment. These contents may be wholesome thoughts, or unwholesome thoughts. In the language of those days, wholesome thoughts were called *kuśala-dharma,* and unwholesome thoughts were called *akuśala-dharma.* We find that these two words were used for a long time in our ancient literature. *Kuśala-dharma* and *akuśala-dharma* are both Dharma. What one's mind contains at this moment is Dharma—*"Dhāretī ti dharma."*

Two other words that occur in the ancient literature are

ārya-dharma and *anārya-dharma.* As the centuries passed, the real meaning of these words has been lost. Today the word *ārya* is used for a particular race of human beings. In the India of those days, this meaning was nowhere to be found. *Ārya* had nothing to do with a race of human beings. Rather, it meant one who has a pure mind—one who is a noble person, a saintly person; one who has eradicated all the impurities of the mind. Such a one was called an *ārya.* One who lives the life of negativity, impurity, and generates anger, hatred, ill will, or animosity, was called *anārya.* So anybody whose mind contained purity was called *ārya,* and anybody whose mind contained impurity was called *anārya.*

Words like Hindu-dharma, Buddhist-dharma or Jain-dharma, were never used in our ancient literature. Other sects came much later, but even when these three were there, nobody used these words. The words *kuśala-dharma* and *akuśala-dharma* were used. Slowly, after a few centuries, another division came: *kuśala-dharma* (wholesome Dharma) was called *dharma,* and *akuśala-dharma* (unwholesome Dharma) was called *adharma.*

In the ancient scriptures, there was another definition of the word *dharma:* the nature or characteristic of what the mind contains, whether wholesome or unwholesome. What is the characteristic of the contents of one's mind? This was called *dharma.* Its nature, its characteristic was called *dharma.* In Indian languages today, we still hear an echo of this meaning when someone says: "The *dharma* of fire is to burn." The nature of fire is to burn itself and to burn others. Similarly, we can say that the *dharma* of ice is to create coolness. This is the nature of ice.

What do these universal characteristics have to do with Hinduism? What have they to do with Buddhism, or Christianity, Islam, Jainism or Sikhism? Fire burns; ice cools. This is a universal law of nature. If fire does not burn itself and others, it cannot be fire. If it is fire, then its characteristic must be to burn itself and to burn others. The *dharma* of the sun is to give light and heat. If it does not give light and heat, it cannot be the sun. The *dharma* of the moon is to give a soft, cool light. This is the *dharma,* the nature of the moon. If it does not do that, it is not the moon.

This was how the word *dharma* was used in those days. If the contents of my mind are unwholesome—for example, if I am generating anger, hatred, ill will, or animosity at this moment—then the nature of these negativities is to burn. They will burn me. The vessel containing the fire is the fire's first victim; then this fire and its heat start spreading to the environment around it.

It is the same when there is negativity in the mind. One who contains this negativity, who generates this negativity, is the first victim. He or she becomes very miserable. How can you expect peace, harmony and happiness, if you are generating anger? This is totally against the law of nature. That means it is totally against Dharma, which is the universal law of nature. If, knowingly or unknowingly, I place my hand in fire, my hand is bound to burn. The fire does not discriminate. It does not notice whether the hand belongs to a person who calls himself or herself a Hindu, Muslim, Christian, Jain, Sikh or Parsi, or an Indian, American, Russian or Chinese. There is no difference, no discrimination, no partiality; Dharma is Dharma.

In the same way, when my mind is generating purity, the negativities are eradicated. According to the law of nature, when the mind is pure, it is full of love, compassion, sympathetic joy and equanimity. This is the nature of a pure mind. This pure mind may belong to a Hindu or a Christian, or it may belong to an Indian or a Pakistani: it makes no difference at all. If the mind is pure, it must have these qualities. And when the mind is full of love, compassion, goodwill and equanimity, then again, the universal law is such that these contents of the mind have their own nature, their own Dharma. They give so much peace, so much harmony, so much happiness. One may keep calling oneself by any name. He may keep performing this rite or that ritual, this religious ceromony or that religious ceremony. He may have this external appearance or that external appearance. He may believe in this philosophy or that philosophy. It makes no difference at all. Dharma is Dharma.

The moment you defile your mind, the moment you generate any negativity, nature starts punishing you then and there. The punishment doesn't wait until after death. Whatever happens after death will happen then. But what happens now? Anybody who generates anger now will experience nothing but unhappiness and misery. This person may have any name, may be from any caste, from any community, from any sect or from any country: it makes no difference at all. Because one has generated negativity, one is bound to suffer here and now.

Similarly, when you generate purity of mind, when your mind is full of good qualities such as love, compassion and goodwill, nature starts rewarding you here and now. You won't have to wait until the end of your life—you start getting the rewards of a pure mind now. When your mind is full of love, full of compassion, you start experiencing so much peace, harmony and happiness. This is Dharma. It has nothing to do with sectarianism.

Someone who calls himself a very staunch Hindu, a staunch Muslim, a staunch Christian or a staunch Sikh, may be a very good Dharmic person, or may not have any trace of Dharma. Sectarian rites and rituals, sectarian beliefs or philosophies, sectarian religious ceremonies and outward appearances have nothing to do with Dharma. Dharma is totally different. Dharma means what your mind contains now. If what it contains is wholesome, it rewards you. If it is unwholesome, it punishes you.

If this understanding of Dharma becomes more and more prevalent in Indian society, as it was twenty-five centuries ago, then the country will be more peaceful because its people will be more peaceful. Everyone will give importance to whether or not he or she is a Dharmic person. That means, is one keeping one's mind pure, free from impurities, free from negativities? If you keep generating anger, hatred, ill will, animosity and other negativities, you are not a Dharmic person.

You may perform some rite or ritual. You may go to a temple and bow before a particular idol, or to a mosque to recite a namaz. You may go to a church to say prayers, or to a gurudwārā to chant kirtans. Or you may go to a pagoda and pay respect to the statue of Buddha. These do not help at all.

When you generate negativity in your mind, you may blame various outside reasons for your misery. You may find fault with others. You may be under the wrong impression that you are miserable because so-and-so abused or insulted you, or because something which you wanted has not happened, or because something that you did not want has happened. You remain deluded for your whole life that you are miserable because of these apparent external reasons. Because Dharma was lost to the country, we have forgotten to go deep inside to find the real cause of misery.

Suppose someone abuses me, and I become miserable. Between these two events, something very important happens inside me. But that link remains unknown to me. When somebody abuses me, I start generating anger and hatred; I start reacting with negativity. Only then do I become miserable, not before. The reason I am miserable is not because somebody has abused me, nor because something unwanted has happened. Rather, it is because I am reacting to these outside things. This is the real cause of my misery. You cannot understand this by listening to discourses such as this, by reading scriptures, by intellectualizing or accepting it at the emotional or devotional level. The real understanding of Dharma can only come when you start experiencing it within yourself.

To illustrate this point: suppose by mistake I have placed my hand in fire. The law of nature is such that the fire starts burning my hand. I take my hand away because I don't like being burned. The next time, I again make a mistake and put my hand in the fire. Again, my hand gets burned, and again I take my hand back. I may do this once, twice, or three times, and then I start to understand: "This is fire, and the nature of fire is to burn. So I had better not touch the fire." This becomes a lesson, and I begin to understand at the experiential level that I must keep my hand away from fire.

In a similar way, one can learn how to practise Dharma using a technique which was very common in ancient India. To learn Dharma means to observe the reality within oneself. The word that was used for this was *"vipassanā,"* which means "to observe reality in a special way." This means to observe reality in the right way, the correct way, to observe it *as it is*—not just as it appears to be, not just as it seems to be, not coloured by any belief or philosophy, not coloured by any imagination—but to observe it by working in a scientific way.

For example, when anger has arisen, you observe the reality that anger has arisen. Cutting yourself off from the external object of anger, you simply observe anger as anger, hatred as hatred; or passion as passion, ego as ego. You observe any impurity that has arisen on the mind. You simply observe it, observe it objectively, without identifying yourself with that particular negativity.

It is very difficult to observe objectively. When anger arises, it is like a volcanic eruption, and we get overpowered by it. When we are overpowered by anger, we cannot observe anger. Instead, we perform all the vocal and physical actions which we did not want to perform. And then we keep repenting: "I should not have done this. I should not have reacted in this way." But the next time a similar situation occurs, we will react in the same way, because we have not experienced the truth within ourselves.

If you learn this technique of observing the reality within yourself, then you will notice that, as anger arises in the mind, two things start happening simultaneously at the physical level. At a gross level—at the level of your breath—you will notice that, as soon as anger, hatred, ill will, passion, ego, or any impurity arises in the mind, your breath loses its normality. It cannot remain normal. It will become abnormal—slightly hard, slightly fast. And once that particular negativity has gone away, you will notice that your breath becomes normal. It is no longer fast, no longer hard. This happens in the physical structure at a gross level.

Something also happens at a subtler level, because mind and matter are so interrelated. One keeps influencing the other, and getting influenced by the other. This interaction is continuously happening within ourselves, day and night. At a subtler level a biochemical reaction starts within the physical structure. An electromagnetic reaction starts and, if you are a good Vipassana meditator, you will notice: "Look, anger has arisen." And then what happens? There is heat throughout the body; there is palpitation; there is tension throughout the body.

One need not do anything except observe. Do nothing; just observe. Don't try to push out your anger. Don't try to push out the signs of the anger. Just observe, just observe. Continue to observe, and you will notice that the anger becomes weaker and weaker, and passes away. If you suppress it, then it goes deep into the subconscious level of your mind. When it is suppressed, it does not pass away.

Whenever misery comes, we think that the cause of this misery is something outside, and we make a great effort to rectify external things: "So-and-so is misbehaving. I am unhappy because of this person's misbehaviour. When this person stops misbehaving, I will be a very happy person." We want to change this person. Is this possible? Can we change others? Well, even if we succeed in changing one person, what guarantee is there that somebody else will not appear, who will again go totally against our desires? It is impossible to change the entire world. The saints and sages, enlightened people, discovered the way out: change yourself. Let anything happen outside, but do not react. Observe the truth as it is. But when we don't know the technique of observing ourselves— the technique of self-realization, the technique of truth-realization—then we can't work out our own salvation.

For example, you may try to divert your attention. You are very miserable and you can't change the other person or the outside situation, so you try to divert your mind. You go to a cinema or a theatre, or worse, to a bar or gambling casino, to divert your attention. For awhile you may feel that your misery is gone. This is an illusion: you have not come out of your misery; it is still there. You have merely diverted your attention, and the misery has gone deep inside. Time and time again it will erupt and overpower you. You have not come out of your misery.

There is another way of diverting the mind, this time in the name of religion. You go to a temple, a mosque, a gurudwārā, or a pagoda, to chant or pray. Your mind will be diverted, and you may feel quite happy. But again, this is an escape. You are not facing your problem. This was not the Dharma of ancient India.

We have to face the problem. When misery arises in the mind, face it. By observing it objectively, you go to the deepest cause of misery. If you can learn to observe the deepest cause of misery, you will find that layers of this deep-rooted cause start getting eradicated. As layer after layer gets peeled off, you start to be relieved of your misery. You have neither suppressed your negativity, nor expressed it at the vocal or physical level and harmed others. You have observed it. Doing nothing, you have just observed.

This is a wonderful technique of India. Unfortunately, our country lost it because we lost the real meaning of the word *dharma*. Now these crutches, these scaffoldings of Hindu-dharma, Buddhist-dharma, Jain-dharma and Muslim-dharma have become predominant for us. When we say Hindu-dharma, then Hindu is predominant for us. Poor Dharma recedes behind the curtain into the darkness. Dharma has no value, because Hindu is more important. When we say Muslim-dharma, Muslim is important. When we say Buddhist-dharma, Buddhist is important; Jain-dharma, Jain is important. It's as if Dharma is not an entity of its own. But what a great entity Dharma is! It is the law of nature, the eternal truth; and we are missing it when we give prominence to these false scaffoldings, crutches. We are forgetting the real essence of Dharma.

When someone starts giving importance to Hindu-dharma, he never gives importance to Dharma. Hindu-dharma and all the rites, rituals, ceremonies and appearances become more important for this person. He performs them and feels that he is a very Dharmic person. Similarly, if one gives importance to Muslim-dharma, Sikh-dharma, or Buddhist-dharma, one feels that he is a very Dharmic person. This person may not have even a trace of Dharma, because all the time his mind is full of impurity, full of negativity. What a great delusion it is when one feels that he is a Dharmic person because he has performed his rite or ritual; because he has gone to this temple or to that mosque; because he has gone to this church or to that gurudwārā; because he has recited this or recited that. What has happened to us? Where is this sectarianism leading us? Far away from Dharma!

The yardstick of Dharma should be: "Is my mind getting purified or not?" There is nothing wrong with performing a particular rite, ritual, or religious ceremony. There is nothing wrong with going to a mosque or a temple. But one should keep examining oneself to see: "Is my mind getting purified by performing all these rites, rituals and ceremonies? Am I getting liberated from anger, hatred, ill will, animosity, passion, ego?" If so, then yes, they are very good.

If no improvement is coming, then one sees that he is just deluding himself, fooling himself: "Even if my mind appears to be purified for a short time, I am deluding myself, because I have not come out of my misery, my impurities. My impurities lie at the deepest unconscious level of my mind. That is the storehouse of my impurities." We carry this storehouse from life to life, from life to life. And we either give more input, more impurities, or we remove them.

Mostly we keep giving more and more input, and therefore we become more and more miserable. How can we purify the deepest level of the mind? We can purify the surface of the mind to some extent by intellectualizing, or by devotional or emotional beliefs. But to take out the impurities from the deepest level of the mind, we have to work—and work in the way that nature wants us to work. The law of nature says that whenever we generate any impurity, the source of the impurity lies at the deepest level of our mind. And the deepest level of our mind is constantly in contact with body sensations.

Day and night, whether you are asleep or awake, the deepest level of your mind (the so-called "unconscious") is never unconscious: it is always feeling sensations on the body. Whenever there is a pleasant sensation, it will react with craving—*rāga, rāga*. Whenever there is an unpleasant sensation, it will react with aversion—*dveṣha, dveṣha*. Craving, aversion, craving, aversion: this has become the behaviour pattern of the mind deep inside. Twenty-four hours a day, day and night, every moment there are sensations in the body deep inside, and at the deepest level the mind keeps reacting. It has become a slave of its own behaviour pattern. Unless we break that slavery, how can we come out of our misery? We will be just deluding ourselves by trying to purify the surface of the mind, while we forget the deep root. As long as the roots are impure, the mind can never become pure.

Vipassana is a technique of India. Laudable references to Vipassana are given in the *Rg Veda*. The most ancient literature of this country is full of words of praise for Vipassana:

Yo viśvābhih vipaśyati bhuvanah

sañca paśyati sa na pārśadati dviśah.

One who practises Vipassana in a perfect way—*sañca paśyati, sa na pārśadati dviśah*—comes out of all aversion and anger; the mind becomes pure.

But one has to practise it oneself. If you just keep reciting this verse of the *Rg Veda*, how is this going to help? Suppose you keep reciting: "The cake is very sweet; the cake is very sweet." How can you taste the sweetness of the cake unless you put it in your mouth? The *practice* of Dharma is more important than merely accepting Dharma at the intellectual, emotional or devotional level. And this practice is Vipassana.

In ancient days, Vipassana was everywhere in India. A traveller came from Burma then. Travelling the whole country, he found that in every household people were practising Vipassana. He visited different households, rich and poor, and found that not only the husband, wife and children, but even the servants were practising Vipassana every morning and evening. And everywhere there was talk of Vipassana, because people were getting benefit from it. Over time, unfortunately, in this country we became involved in rites, rituals and religious ceremonies and forgot this scientific understanding of Dharma.

Dharma is nothing but a pure science, a super-science of mind and matter: the interaction of mind and matter, the cross-currents and the under-currents happening deep inside every moment. Things are happening inside every moment, but we remain extroverted, giving importance to things outside. Say somebody has abused me, and I don't have this practice of observing what is happening within myself: I become angry and start shouting. What am I doing?

When someone is abusing me, it is that person's problem, not mine. If they are abusing, it means that they are generating negativity in the mind. This person is a sick person, an unhappy person, a miserable person when he is generating anger and shouting. Why should I generate anger? Why should I shout and make myself miserable? This understanding cannot come unless you have experienced it. It is like the experience when you touch fire and learn not to touch it again. It happens once, twice, several times, and then you learn not to touch fire again. Similarly, you can develop the ability to observe what is happening inside. Anger has arisen and you will immediately notice that there is fire, and it has started burning you: "Look, I am burning! I don't like burning. Next time I will be more careful." Or, "Oh no, here is anger. If I generate anger, I'll burn." By mistake you have again generated anger; again you observe it. Again you generate anger, and again you observe it. After a few experiences, you start coming out of it.

But when you are not observing the reality within yourself, then you give all importance to the apparent external cause of your misery, trying to rectify that. For example, a mother-in-law says: "Our household is a real hell now." If you ask her the reason, she says: "It is all because of this daughter-in-law. What a daughter-in-law has come into our house! She is so modernized. She goes totally against all our traditions and beliefs! She has spoiled the entire harmony of the household." If you talk to the daughter-in-law, she will say: "The old lady should change a little. She doesn't understand that there is a generation gap. The times are changing. Why doesn't she understand? She is making herself and everybody else miserable." The daughter-in-law wants the mother-in-law to change. The mother-in-law wants the daughter-in-law to change. The father wants the son to change. The son wants the father to change. This brother wants the other brother to change. The other brother wants this brother to change.

"I won't change. I am perfectly all right. Nothing in me needs changing!" We never see within ourselves that we are *not* perfectly all right, that we are the cause of our own misery. The basic problem lies within ourselves, not outside. We start realizing this at the experiential level by practising Vipassana. It is very difficult to observe abstract anger. Even for a Vipassana meditator, it takes a long time before one reaches the stage where one can observe abstract anger, or abstract passion, abstract fear, abstract ego. It is very difficult.

When anger arises, along with it, a sensation starts in the body. Along with anger, the breath also becomes abnormal. You can observe this. Even in ten days you can learn this technique. By coming to a Vipassana course and working properly, you can understand how to observe the breath. Perhaps anger has come, and you can't observe abstract anger, but you can observe your breath: "Look, the breath is coming in and going out." This is not a breathing exercise. You just observe the breath as it is—if it is shallow, it is shallow; if it is deep, it is deep; if it passes through the left nostril, then the left nostril; through the right nostril, then the right nostril. You simply observe it. Or perhaps there is heat throughout the body, or palpitation, or tension. You just observe them. It is easy. These things become easy to observe if you practise even for one or two ten-day courses.

To observe anger as anger, or hatred as hatred, or passion as passion, is very difficult. It takes time. That is why the wise people, the enlightened people, the saints and seers of India advised: "Observe yourself." Observing oneself is a path of self-realization, truth-realization—one can even say "God-realization," because after all, truth is God. What else is God? The law is God, nature is God. And when one is observing that law; one is observing Dharma. Whatever is happening within you, you are just a silent observer, not reacting. As you observe objectively, you have started taking the first step to understand Dharma; the first step towards practising Dharma in life.

By practising Dharma, you won't run away from external activities like going to this or that temple, or performing this or that rite or ritual. But at the same time as you are doing these things, you will start observing the reality pertaining to your mind at that moment: "What is happening in my mind at this moment? Whatever is happening in my mind from moment to moment—this is more important for me than anything that is happening outside." You will start to notice how are you reacting to things outside. Whenever you react, this reaction becomes a source of misery for you If you learn not to react but simply to observe, you will come out of the suffering. Of course it takes time. One does not become perfect immediately, but a beginning is made.

Let a beginning be made to understand Dharma. Dharma is free from all sectarian beliefs, dogmas, rites and rituals. Even sectarian names are not necessary. You may or may not call yourself a Hindu or a Muslim, but you should be a Dharmic person, a person living the life of Dharma. This means that your mind should remain pure. If your mind remains pure, then all your other actions, vocal or physical, will naturally become pure.

Mind is the base. When the mind is impure, full of negativities, then our vocal actions are bound to be impure, and our physical actions are bound to be impure. We have started harming ourselves. We have started harming others. As I said, when you generate anger, or hatred, or ill will, you are the first victim of your negativity. You become very miserable, and the misery that you generate because of your negativity starts to permeate the atmosphere around you. The entire environment around you becomes so tense. Anyone who comes in contact with you at that time becomes tense, miserable. You are distributing your misery to others. This is what you have, and you keep distributing it to others. You are making yourself miserable, and you are making others miserable.

On the other hand, if you learn the art of Dharma—this means the art of living—and you stop generating negativity, you start experiencing peace and harmony within yourself. When you keep your mind pure, full of love and compassion, the peace and harmony that is generated within permeates the atmosphere around you. Anyone who comes in contact with you at that time starts experiencing peace and harmony. You are distributing something good that you have. You have peace, you have harmony, you have real happiness, and you are distributing this to others. This is Dharma, the art of living.

In ancient India, Dharma was nothing but an art of living, the art of how to live peacefully and harmoniously within, and how to generate nothing but peace and harmony for others. And to achieve that, proper training was given. There were Vipassana meditation centres in practically every village. Vipassana centres were everywhere, as were yoga schools, yoga colleges and yoga hospitals. They were a part of life. Students used to learn this art in their schooling. Practising it, they lived good lives, healthy lives, harmonious lives.

May that era come again. May people understand what Dharma is. May you be released from the demons, the devils, of sectarianism and communalism which make you forget all about Dharma. May you come out of this suffering. May you live a real life of Dharma, so peaceful, harmonious and happy for you and so peaceful, harmonious and happy for others.

May all of you who have come to this Dharma talk find time to spare ten days of your life to learn this technique. You will get the benefits here and now. It is not necessary for you to convert yourself from one organized religion to another organized religion, from one sect to another sect. Let a Hindu keep calling him or herself Hindu for the whole life. Let a Christian keep calling himself Christian for the whole life—a Muslim, Muslim; a Sikh, Sikh; a Buddhist, Buddhist. But one should become a good Hindu. One should become a good Muslim, a good Christian, a good Sikh, a good Buddhist. One should become a good human being. Dharma teaches you how to become a good human being, how to live a good life, a happy life, a harmonious life.

May all of you get trained in this wonderful technique. Come out of your misery and enjoy real peace, real harmony, real happiness. Real happiness to you all. Real happiness to you all.

Questions and Answers

Q: How can we avoid karma?

A: Be the master of your own mind. The whole technique teaches you how to become your own master. If you are not the master of your mind, then because of the old habit pattern, you will keep on performing those actions, that karma, which you don't want to perform. Intellectually you understand: "I should not perform these actions." Yet you still perform them, because you do not have mastery over your mind. This technique will help you to become the master of your own mind.

Q: What is the ultimate goal of life? That is, what does all this harmony lead to?

A: The ultimate life, the ultimate goal, is here and now. If you keep looking for something in the future but you don't gain anything now, this is a delusion. If you have started experiencing peace and harmony now, then there is every likelihood that you will reach the goal, which is nothing but peace and harmony. So experience it now, at this moment. Then you are really on the right path.

Q: How can a truly Dharmic person face this adharmic world?

A: Don't try to change the adharmic world. Try to change the adharma in yourself, the way in which you are reacting and making yourself miserable. As I said, when somebody is abusing you, understand that this person is miserable. It is the problem of that person. Why make it your problem? Why start generating anger and becoming miserable? Doing that means you are not your own master, you are that person's slave; whenever that person wants to, he can make you miserable. You are the slave of someone else who is a miserable person. You have not understood Dharma. Be your own master and you can live a Dharmic life in spite of the adharmic situations all around.

Q: **Is there any shorter way?**

A: I would say this is the shortest way. You have to change your habit pattern; you have to go to the root of your problem. And the root of problem is inside, not outside. If you learn how to take a dip inside, if you start changing things at the root level, this is the shortest way for you to come out of your misery.

Q: **Some people have impurities, but they feel happy and don't look miserable. Please explain.**

A: You have not entered the minds of these people. A person may have alot of money, and others may feel: "Such a happy person. Look, he has so much wealth." But what you don't know is that this person can't get sound sleep; he has to use sleeping pills—a very miserable person. You can know for yourself how miserable you are, going deep inside. You can't understand at the external level by seeing sombody's face whether he or she is miserable or happy. The misery lies deep inside.

Q: **What is the Dharma of *ātma*, soul?**

A: Observe yourself and you will find what is happening inside. What you call "soul," what you call *ātma*, you will notice, is just a reacting mind, a certain part of the mind. Yet you remain under the illusion that: "This is 'I.' See, this is 'I,' this is 'I.'" This illusion of 'I' will go away, and then the reaction will go away, and you will be liberated from your misery. This does not happen by accepting philosophical beliefs.

Q: **How to deal with insomnia?**

A: Vipassana will help you. When people can't sleep properly, if they lie down and observe respiration or sensations, they can get sound sleep. Even if they don't get sound sleep, the next day they will get up feeling very fresh, as if they have come out of a deep sleep. Practise. Try, and you will find that it is very helpful.

Q: What is the relevance of Dharma to a person on the street, whose stomach is empty?

A: A large number of people living in slums come to Vipassana courses and find it very helpful. Their stomachs are empty, but theirs mind also are so agitated. With such agitated minds, they can't solve their daily problems. With Vipassana, they learn how to keep their minds calm and equanimous. Then they can face their problems. They get better results in their lives. Moreover, I have found that, although people from the slums are very poor, most of their earnings is spent on alcohol and gambling. After taking a few courses, they come out of gambling, they come out of alcohol; they come out of all kinds of addictions. Dharma is helpful. It is helpful to one and all, rich or poor. It makes no difference.

Q: What is the effect of Vipassana on the chakras of the subtle body?

A: *Chakras* are nothing but nerve centres on the spinal chord. Vipassana takes you to the stage where you can feel activity in every little atom of your body. *Chakras* are just a part of that. This activity can be experienced in the entire body.

Q: How do you define eternal life in your meditation system?

A: It is not my meditation system! It is an Indian meditation system, ancient India's meditation system. The life is eternal, but you have to make it purified, so that you live a better life, a good life. Don't try to find the beginning of life, when it started—what you will gain by that? The life is starting every moment; this ball is rolling. It is rolling in a wrong way, and you are a miserable person. Come out of that misery. That is more important than anything else.

Q: How does one escape from anger?

A: This is what Vipassana will teach you. Observe your anger, and you will come out of it. And to observe anger, you learn how to observe your respiration, and how to observe your sensations.

Q: **How can professionals, who have less time, practise meditation?**

A: Meditation is all the more important for professionals! Those who are householders, who have responsibilities in life, need Vipassana much more, because they have to face situations in life where there are so many vicissitudes. They become agitated because of these vicissitudes. If they learn Vipassana, they can face life much better. They can make good decisions, right decisions, correct decisions, which will be very helpful to them. For professionals, executives, and other people with responsibilities, Vipassana is a great boon.

Q: **Do you believe in rebirth?**

A: My believing or not believing will not help you. Meditate, and you will reach a stage where you can see your past, and you can see your future. Then only believe. Don't believe something just because your guru says so. Otherwise you will be under the clutches of a guru, which is against Dharma.

Q: **What is mind? Where it is?**

A: This is what you will understand by practising Vipassana. You will make an analytical study of your mind, an analytical study of your matter, and the interaction between the two.

Q: **How can we make others peaceful?**

A: Make yourself peaceful! Only then you can make others peaceful.

Q: **I agree that this meditation will help me, but how does it solve the problems of society?**

A: Society is, after all, nothing but a group of individuals. We want to solve the problems of society, yet we don't solve the problems of the individual. We want peace in the world, yet we do nothing for the peace of the individual. How is this possible? If each individual experiences peace and harmony, then we will find that the whole society starts experiencing peace and harmony.

Q: **I can't suppress my anger, even if I try.**

A: Don't suppress it: observe it! If you suppress it, problems will come. The more you try to suppress the anger, the more it goes to the deeper level of your mind. The complexes become stronger and stronger, and it is so difficult to come out of them. Just observe your anger. No suppression, no expression. Just observe.

Q: **Are anger and observation simultaneous, or is observation a process arising after thought?**

A: No, it is not a thought. You observe simultaneously, as the anger arises.

Q: **If someone is purposely making our life miserable—how to tolerate this?**

A: First of all, don't try to change the other person. Try to change yourself. Somebody is trying to make you miserable. But you are becoming miserable because you are reacting to this. If you learn how to observe your reaction, then nobody can make you miserable. Any amount of misery from others cannot make you miserable if you learn to remain equanimous deep inside. This technique will help you. Once you become free from misery deep inside, this will also start affecting others. The same person who was harming you will start changing little by little.

Q: **Isn't excusing a sinner encouraging sin?**

A: Never encourage sin. Stop people from committing sin. But don't have aversion or anger towards the sinner. Have love, have compassion. This person is a miserable person, an ignorant person, who doesn't know what he or she is doing. They are harming themselves and harming others. So you use all your strength, physical and vocal, to stop this person from committing sin, but with love and compassion towards them. This is what Vipassana will teach you.

Q: **Can we get complete transformation and complete happiness through Vipassana?**

A: It is a progressive process. As you start working, you will find that you are experiencing more and more happiness, and eventually you will reach the stage which is total happiness. You become more and more transformed, and you will reach the stage which is total transformation. It is progressive.

Q: What is superior to mind?

A: First know what mind is. Then you will know what is beyond mind, what is superior to mind.

Q: How do you equate religion and Dharma?

A: Well, if religion is taken as Hindu religion or Buddhist religion, and so on, then it is totally against Dharma. But if religion is taken as the law of nature, the universal law of nature, then it is the same as Dharma.

Q: How much should we practise Vipassana in our daily life?

A: Take a course, and then you will understand how to apply the practice in your life. If you just take a course and don't apply it in life, then Vipassana will become just a rite, ritual, or a religious ceremony. It won't help you. Vipassana is to live a good life. You will understand how to apply it in life after taking a course.

Q: What is depression? Is it an external, or an internal, problem?

A: All problems are internal. There are no external problems. If you go deep inside and discover the cause of your misery, you will find that every cause lies within yourself, not outside. Remove that cause, and you will be free from misery.

Q: What is the difference between Dharma and duty?

A: Whatever is helpful to you and helpful to others is your duty, is Dharma. Whatever is harmful to you and harmful to others is not your duty, because it harms you and also harms others.

Q: Suffering, war and conflict are as old as history. Do you really believe in a world of peace?

A: Well, even if a few people come out of misery, it is good. When there is darkness all around and one lamp has started giving light, it is good. And like this, if one lamp becomes ten lamps, or twenty lamps, the darkness will get dispelled here and there. There is no guarantee that the entire world will become peaceful, but as much peace as you make in yourself, that much you are helping the peace of the world.

Day Two:
Living the Life of Morality and
Developing Mastery over the Mind

Day Two:
Living the Life of Morality and Developing Mastery over the Mind

Friends: We have assembled here again this evening to further discuss the subject of Dharma. Yesterday we discussed Dharma and sectarianism. Unfortunately in India today, these two words have become synonymous, which is totally wrong. The two are poles apart. Dharma is its own entity. Dharma is universal. It is all-powerful. Dharma is the law of nature, the universal law of nature which governs the entire universe. All animate and inanimate beings are governed by the law of Dharma.

The Dharma of the negativities of the mind is to make one miserable. This law existed in the past, this law exists today and this law will still exist in the future. It is eternal. The Dharma of the purity of the mind has the qualities of love, compassion and goodwill. It gives peace and harmony. This was so in the past, it is so today and it will be so in future. This is the reason why Dharma is *sanātana*—eternal. Unfortunately today, even this Hindi word *sanātana* has become sectarian. *Sanātana Dharma* means a particular Dharma of a particular sect. It is a great misfortune that India has lost the real meaning of Dharma. Because of this, it has become very difficult for people to practise Dharma.

Dharma and sectarianism are totally different. When the country became independent, some very wise, experienced, patriotic people framed the Constitution and declared: "Our government will be a secular government." This was a good thing: a good government is always a secular government. But in Hindi, the word is used in a very wrong way. We say: "Our government is *Dharma nirapeksha.*" How can it be *Dharma nirapeksha? Nirapeksha* means indifferent or unconcerned. The idea is to be *sampradāya nirapeksha—* not favouring any sect. How can a *Dharma nirapeksha* government administer a country? A government has to be *Dharma sāpeksha:* secular, non-sectarian. A government has to have Dharma, otherwise what kind of government will it be? Dharma has to be there.

A state administration has to be an administration of Dharma. By saying that the state, or the administration, or the government is *Dharma nirapeksha,* we have lost the meaning of the word Dharma. For us, Dharma has become a sect. That is why we say "Hindu-dharma, Buddhist-dharma, Jain-dharma" and "Muslim-dharma." Actually we should be saying "Hindu sect, Buddhist sect, Jain sect" and "Muslim sect." Dharma is totally different from these sects, totally different. Sects are limited. Dharma is universal, boundless, infinite and limitless. Dharma is for all, for everyone. This must be very clear. The sooner our country starts understanding the difference between Dharma and sect, the easier it will become for people to practise Dharma. Otherwise they will remain under the illusion that they are Dharmic people when actually they are not. This is a great self-deception. When people do not follow Dharma, they do not get the benefit of Dharma.

The first basic prerequisite of Dharma is to live a moral life. Morality is the base of Dharma. Someone calling oneself a staunch Hindu, or Muslim, Christian, Buddhist or Jain, may not live the life of morality, yet still calls himself a staunch Hindu (etc.) because he performs the rites and rituals of that particular sect, that particular tradition. Morality is missing. Someone who calls himself a Dharmic person must be living a moral life. Without the base of morality, one can never be a Dharmic person, a Dharmist person.

What is morality? Consider our country's penal code: If you kill someone, you are penalized. If you steal something which does not belong to you, you are penalized. If you commit rape or adultery, you are penalized. If you speak lies and deceive somebody, you are penalized. If you become intoxicated and harm others, you are penalized. All these are a part of Dharma, a life of morality. Morality is the essential prerequisite of Dharma. In the ancient language, it was called *sīla*. *Sīla* means "morality." In the past, what explanation did the enlightened ones, the liberated ones, the wise ones, give for this word? They said that one should not perform any action, physical or vocal, which disturbs the peace and harmony of others. One should not perform any action, physical or vocal, which harms other beings, which hurts other beings. This is *sīla*. This is morality.

If we start understanding this, then we may keep calling ourselves Hindu. There is nothing wrong with this. Just as one might call oneself Goenka, Rao, Smith or Jones, we may call ourselves Muslim, Jain, Christian or Buddhist. These are just names. But Dharma is different. If I am a Dharmic person, I must try my best to live a life of morality. As much morality as I have in my life, that much I am a Dharmic person. This name or that name makes no difference. We must abstain from all those physical and vocal actions which go against the interest of other beings. This means we must abstain from killing, from stealing, from sexual misconduct, and from speaking lies. Long ago, in ancient India, these were the four important moral bases. People followed four moral precepts in their lives. Later on, people discovered some intoxicants, like alcohol and marijuana, and started using them. Wise people said: "Once you take any kind of intoxicant, even though you want to live a moral life, it becomes very difficult because you have become the slave of that intoxicant." Therefore, the fifth moral precept was added: abstention from taking any kind of intoxicant. The four precepts became five precepts—five *sīlas*.

Time passed, and slowly people realized that intoxication is not merely the intoxication of alcohol, marijuana, or *bhāng*, and so on; there is also the intoxication of gambling. Therefore the moral precept to abstain from gambling was added. More time passed, and people realized that a bigger intoxication is that of wealth, power and status. Once one accumulates wealth, he becomes quite mad, performing actions which are harmful to himself, and harmful to others. The accumulation of wealth can also be an intoxicant. As a householder one has to work hard to earn money. There is nothing wrong with that. A householder should not be a beggar; therefore one must earn one's living honestly by hard work. This is Dharma. But once you start working hard and earning money, there is a danger that you may get intoxicated with that money. You may get trapped in the rat race of accumulating more and more money. A dangerous situation.

The householder faces a dilemma. On the one hand, a householder needs to earn money to support himself or herself, the members of one's family, and the other members of society. Yet on the other hand, there is the danger of becoming intoxicated by this. So, the rule of *samvibhāga* was made. *Samvibhāga* is a word from the ancient Indian language, most of which we have lost today. It has gone to neighbouring countries and is preserved there. In those days the word *dāna*—donation—was not used. When you give *dāna*, your ego becomes strong: "I am giving *dāna*." So instead of *dāna*, they used *samvibhāga*, which means the money that comes to you from society. The money that you accumulated came from society—now distribute it to society. *Samvibhāga:* share it with other people. Share it with those who need it. *Samvibhāga* was a part of the five precepts.

The five precepts were essential. They are still essential. They are the basic prerequisites of Dharma, and they will remain essential in future also as the basic prerequisites of Dharma. One yardstick to measure whether one is a Dharmic person or not is whether one is living the life of the five precepts. Why observe these five precepts? The enlightened ones explained why *sīla* is necessary. They explained it in different ways to different people, according to the mental calibre of the people to whom they were speaking. In a society, there are people of different mental calibres. Some are like children, some like adolescents, some like youths and some like adults. Explanations were given to different people in different ways.

To some it was explained: "If you observe all these moral precepts very scrupulously, do you know what you will gain? When you die, you will get reborn in heaven." And a description of heaven was given: "A wonderful heaven, with celestial drinks and celestial women..." and so on. Hearing that, a person feels elated: "If I can attain that, certainly I must observe morality. I must observe *sīla*."

Similarly, one might say to one's child: "If you study well in school and do your homework properly, you will get Cadbury's sweets." So the child works hard.

Or it was explained: "If you don't observe these moral precepts, do you know what will happen? After death, you will go to hell." A description of hell was given, so horrible. One gets frightened: "Oh no, I don't want to go to hell!"

The stick and the carrot. There were people who could understand only this kind of language, so they were given these explanations. Whether a person understands by this or that language, if he or she abstains from performing unwholesome actions, it is good for them.

There were other people who were intellectuals. They didn't believe in the next birth, in this heaven or that hell. They believed that this life now is more important. People of that type gave all importance to the present life. For such people, the explanation was given in a different way: "If somebody tried to kill you, would you like it? Would you feel happy about it? Or would you feel unhappy?"

"Oh, I would feel very unhappy if somebody tried to kill me." "Similarly, if you tried to kill somebody, would that person feel unhappy?" "That person would feel unhappy."

"If someone stole something belonging to you, something very dear to you, wouldn't you feel unhappy?" "Certainly I would feel unhappy. That is true."

"If you stole something belonging to somebody else, which was very dear to that person, wouldn't that person feel unhappy?" "Yes, that person would feel unhappy."

"If somebody committed adultery or sexual misconduct

with a member of your family, wouldn't you feel unhappy?" "I certainly would feel unhappy."

"Similarly, if you committed sexual misconduct with someone, wouldn't the members of their family feel unhappy?" "They would feel unhappy."

"If somebody spoke lies and deceived you, wouldn't you feel unhappy?" "I would feel unhappy."

"Similarly, if you tried to deceive others by speaking lies, wouldn't they feel unhappy?" "Yes, they would."

"If somebody got intoxicated, and disturbed your peace and harmony, wouldn't you feel unhappy?" "Yes." "Similarly, if you got intoxicated, and disturbed the peace and harmony of others, wouldn't they feel unhappy?" "Yes, certainly they would."

In this way, one can understand logically, rationally. Many people started understanding Dharma in that way.

Another explanation was given, a different explanation to people of different mental calibres, all for the same good purpose: "A human being is a social being. One has to live in society. One cannot run away from society. A householder has to live with the members of one's household and with the members of society. Even if somebody has renounced the world and become a monk or a nun, one still has to keep in contact with society. A human being is a social being.

"If the peace and harmony of society gets disturbed by any action of yours, do you think you will experience peace and harmony? If you are burning with fire all around you, can you experience peace within yourself? You have to maintain the peace and harmony of society. Any action of yours, physical or vocal, which disturbs the peace and harmony of others, disturbs your peace and harmony also, because you are a member of society. You cannot keep aloof from society." This explanation was logical, rational and understandable.

Then there were many mature people in society, to whom Dharma was explained in a very mature way: "At the apparent level it seems that if you observe *sīla,* the moral precepts—

if you don't harm others, if you don't hurt others by any action, vocal or physical, then you are obliging others and you are obliging society, because you are helping them to live peacefully. But this is only the apparent truth, not the actual truth, not the truth at the deeper level of Dharma. At the deeper level of Dharma, you are not obliging anybody by practising *sīla*, morality. You are obliging yourself. It is in your own self-interest."

To such people, it was explained in this way: "Suppose you kill somebody. How it is possible to kill? You can't kill anybody unless you generate a tremendous amount of anger, hatred, ill will and animosity. You can't kill while smiling or laughing. You have to generate negativity in your mind; and as soon as you generate negativity, nature starts punishing you. You may kill that person later on, but you will be the first victim. You have started harming yourself because you have started generating impurity, negativity in the mind. You can't kill somebody unless you generate negativity."

Similarly, you can't steal unless you generate a tremendous amount of greed in your mind. You can't perform sexual misconduct unless you generate a tremendous amount of lust and passion in your mind. You can't speak a lie unless you generate a tremendous amount of ego, craving or aversion. Only then can you deceive others. When you break any *sīla* at the physical level or the vocal level, you have to generate some impurity or the other in your mind. You have started harming yourself.

When you are this ignorant, you know nothing about Dharma. The law of Dharma says that as soon as you generate any negativity, any impurity in the mind, Dharma will punish you. If you have broken the law of Dharma, you will be punished. And you will be punished here and now, not just after death. The punishment that comes after death will come. That is a separate issue; don't give it much importance. A wise person must give importance to the reality of this moment. What is happening at this moment? The punishment is given here and now.

If a person breaks the law of the country, he or she has to suffer. They receive punishment because they have broken the law. But the determination of the punishment takes time. Investigations go on; the case goes from this court to that court, to another court. It may take years to resolve. And even then, one may not be given any punishment. Those who are responsible to determine proper punishment may start seeing the other side of the case, and the accused person may go free.

But in Dharma, this can never happen. In Dharma, the punishment is immediate and simultaneous. As soon as a negativity arises in the mind, simultaneously misery starts arising in the mind. There is no time gap. It is not that you generate negativity now and after a few moments you will become miserable. You become miserable at that very moment. Nature has started punishing you. You can't avoid this punishment. You have to face it.

Because people have forgotten the meaning of Dharma, it is not understood as the law of nature. Dharma is understood as Hindu-dharma, Buddhist-dharma or Jain-dharma; this rite or that rite, this religion or that religion; this recitation or that recitation, this ceremony or that ceremony—all of which have nothing to do with Dharma. The law of nature is the law of nature, the universal law of nature. If this becomes clear to society and to the country, a big change will start coming and everybody will give importance to the law of nature.

What am I doing at this moment? Am I generating any negativity in my mind? If so, nature has started punishing me. If I keep myself free from negativity, I don't generate negativity. If I don't perform any action, physical or vocal, which disturbs others, I don't generate negativity in my mind. If I don't generate negativity, my mind becomes pure and nature starts rewarding me here and now. The moment a pure mind starts generating love, compassion and goodwill, simultaneously one starts experiencing peace, harmony and happiness. You won't have to wait. It's not that you will get something after death. You will get it now—here and now.

This is the law of nature. This is Dharma. The more people

start understanding this, the more they will try to live a life of morality, not to oblige others, but to oblige themselves. If I live a life of morality, I am obliging myself. I am helping myself. And if I help myself, I have certainly started helping others also. When I harm others, I have started harming myself. So in my own self-interest, I have to live a life of morality, I have to live a life of Dharma.

Not Hindu-dharma, Buddhist-dharma, Jain-dharma or Muslim-dharma; they have nothing to do with Dharma. Somebody who calls himself a good Hindu-dharmist, may be a Dharmist or may not be a Dharmist. These are two different things altogether. Dharma is Dharma. If we take Dharma out of this mire of sectarianism, then it will become very pure. People will start understanding Dharma as Dharma, nothing to do with Hindu, Buddhist, Jain, Muslim or Christian. People will start following Dharma, people will start observing Dharma. But how to observe it?

As a mature person, one has understood: "In my own interest, I must live the life of morality. Of course, I must also live the life of morality in the interest of society. I should not kill. I should not steal. I should not perform sexual misconduct. I should not speak lies. I should not get intoxicated."

A drunkard knows very well: "Drinking is no good for me." He wants to come out of it. A gambler understands: "Gambling is no good for me." He wants to come out of it. One who performs sexual misconduct understands: "This is no good for me." He wants to come out of it. Yet when the time comes, still one performs all those actions which one knows are not good.

There is a story in the *Mahābhārata* featuring an important character named Duryodhan. Duryodhan says:

Jānāmi dharmaṃ na ca me pravrittī

jānāmi adharmaṃ na ca me nivrittī.

"I know very well what Dharma is, but my mind does not want to follow it. I know very well what adharma is, and yet I cannot come out of it."

Isn't everyone like Duryodhan? Everyone understands at the intellectual level: "I should not perform any bad actions. I should only perform actions which are good." And yet one keeps performing wrong actions, and does not perform good actions. Everyone is like Duryodhan, because one has no control over the mind.

Therefore the second important prerequisite of Dharma is to develop mastery over the mind. You understand very well: "A moral life is good for me and good for others." You want to live a moral life, and yet you can't, because you have no mastery over your mind. Dharma is not complete without mastery of the mind.

The wise people, the enlightened people, the *rishis*, the *mūnis*, the *buddhas*, the *arahants*, the *sthitaprajñas*, they didn't just give sermons: "Oh, people of the world, you should not kill. You should not steal. You should not do this. You should not do that." If Dharma was only sermons then, as happens today, the words would enter one ear and go out the other ear. The spiritual leaders of India's past didn't give mere sermons. They gave us a way to practise what those sermons taught, and to observe morality by developing mastery over the mind. That is very important. One has to develop mastery over one's mind.

Many methods were used. India is a vast country, a very ancient country. Different techniques were developed and different techniques were practised. One technique is good for some people; another technique is good for others. Different techniques evolved to develop mastery over the mind, to control the mind. How to control the mind? One very popular technique was to keep reciting a word. This practice continues today. As you keep reciting the same word, you will find that the mind gets calmed down and starts getting concentrated. You can use any word—for example, "watch." You keep reciting: "Watch, watch, watch, watch, watch, watch, watch." The mind gets calmed down, concentrated. This is the law of nature. It is like singing a lullaby to a child: "Oh sleep, my child. Oh sleep, my child. Oh sleep, my child." The child calms down and goes to sleep, because you repeated the same words over and over. Similarly, when you repeat: "Watch, watch, watch, watch, watch, watch": the mind calms down and gets concentrated.

It is difficult to repeat a word like: "Watch, watch, watch." What is interesting about repeating this word? So intelligent people advised: "Start repeating the name of any saintly person, any being, any god or goddess in whom you have confidence and devotion. If you have devotion, it becomes easy for you to repeat that word. Keep repeating it." Then a suggestion was given: "This name is so powerful. If you practise repeating it, after death you will get heaven; after death you will get liberated."

It is easy to repeat the name of a god, or a goddess, or a saintly person, enlightened person if you have devotion and faith in that person. As you keep repeating, repeating, repeating it, the mind gets more and more concentrated. It was a very good technique. It worked in the past and works even today.

Another technique was to use a shape or a form, any shape or form. There was a technique in India where a particular shape made from clay—for example, a disk the size of a chapati—was made. Someone would place it in front of oneself, and keep looking at it. One would close his eyes, then with open eyes look at it, then again close the eyes. This very ancient technique of India was called *nimītta*. One looked at the object, closed the eyes, opened the eyes, then closed the eyes. When someone practises this, a time comes when the shape of the clay disk will come in front of them, even with closed eyes. But to give so much importance to a clay disk becomes difficult.

So the instruction was given: Take the shape or form of a particular god or goddess in whom you have faith or devotion—an idol or a picture of this particular god or goddess. Look at it, close your eyes, look at it again, then close your eyes again. Keep practising this. After a few days or a few months, or in some cases maybe a few years, as soon as you close your eyes, the picture will come before you. When the picture comes before you with closed eyes, the mind gets concentrated. It worked in those days; it works even now.

Another technique was to imagine something, to develop faith in that imaginary object, and start working with that. For example, "This is my spinal chord, and there are *chakras* on this spinal chord." You imagine these *chakras*. Or you imagine one *chakra* as a lotus with so many petals, then another *chakra* as a different lotus with so many petals. You keep imagining this again and again, repeatedly, repeatedly. A time will come when you start observing those lotuses easily with closed eyes. As you continue the practice of imagining something, your mind gets concentrated.

The auto-suggestion of any philosophical belief was used. For example, you have a certain belief: "I am the immortal soul. Yes, I am the immortal soul. This immortal soul is very pure. It is very pure. There is no trace of impurity in it." You keep giving yourself this suggestion: "I am immortal. I am the immortal soul." Or: "I am God Almighty. I am God Almighty. I am all-powerful. I am complete purity." You repeatedly give this suggestion. These thoughts will start projecting themselves, and the mind will get concentrated.

Like this, the people of India worked in different ways, with different techniques, to train the mind to get concentrated. That was the main aim: to get the mind concentrated. One person might follow one way, someone else another way, but the objective was the same: to get the mind concentrated.

But then there were also fully enlightened people in our country who realized that mere concentration of the mind is not enough. A concentrated mind is very powerful. When your mind gets concentrated by using this technique or that technique, it becomes a very powerful mind. This powerful mind can be misused: it can harm others. But a powerful mind with the base of purity cannot harm anybody. It will be helpful to everyone. So the base must be pure. If you concentrate your mind without a pure base, it will not give you the proper results of Dharma. Therefore purity is very important.

So other techniques were discovered where the base was purity, nothing but purity. The first condition was to remain with the reality that one experiences—the reality of the moment as it is—and to remain with that reality from moment to moment, from moment to moment; the reality that one realizes oneself, not the reality experienced by somebody else. The reality experienced by Gotama made Gotama a fully enlightened one, a *buddha*. It cannot make you a *buddha* unless you realize it yourself. The reality experienced by Jesus made Jesus the Christ, not you, not anybody else.

Each individual has to experience the truth, the reality. And this reality is the reality only when you experience it yourself. If you have read something in the scriptures—the scriptures say so, or your guru says so, or your tradition says so—and you simply believe it: this won't help. You have to experience it yourself. Truth is the reality that you are experiencing from moment to moment. You can only experience the reality pertaining to yourself. The reality pertaining to others can only be understood at the intellectual level. You can understand an external truth only at the intellectual level: "This is so. It appears to be so. It is like this or like this." You can only intellectualize the external truth.

If you want to experience the truth, then the truth must be within the framework of your body. The reality that you experience within the framework of your body is the reality for you. It is your reality; you are experiencing it. It is a reality not because your guru says so, or your scriptures say so, or your tradition says so, but because you are experiencing it. So start with the truth pertaining to yourself, as experienced by you, within yourself. Make use of concentration of mind. The training of mental concentration should start with the experience of the truth pertaining to yourself. This is the truth pertaining to the physical structure, the material structure, the corporeal structure, which one keeps understanding as, "I, I; mine, mine." At the intellectual level, one understands very well: "This body is not 'I,' this body is not 'mine,' this body is not 'my soul.'" One understands this very well at the intellectual level.

When you start practising the observation of the truth within yourself, you will notice that, for all practical purposes, this material body has become "I" for you, has become "mine" for you: "It is 'I,' it is 'mine'; it is 'I,' it is 'mine.'" There is a tremendous amount of identification with this body and a tremendous amount of attachment towards this body. Because of this, there is a tremendous amount of misery and a tremendous amount of tension. The reality pertaining to the physical structure, and similarly, the reality pertaining to the mental structure have to be realized.

What is this mind to which I keep saying: "I, I; mine, mine"? What is this mind? At the intellectual level, I may keep on saying: "The mind is not 'I,' the mind is not 'mine,' the mind is not 'my soul.' " But at the actual level, the mind has become "I." the mind has become "mine." What is this mind? One has to explore for oneself the truth pertaining to the body, the truth pertaining to the mind, within oneself, at the experiential level.

For this a technique was given. The first instructions are to sit comfortably in any posture that suits you. It is not necessary to sit in this particular posture, or that particular posture. Any posture that keeps you comfortable for longer periods at a stretch is a good posture for you. Try to keep your back and your neck straight. Close your eyes, close your mouth, and then see what is happening within the framework of the body. Observe whatever you are experiencing at the experiential level, with no imagination, no speculation. At this moment, what are you experiencing? There is no vocal activity and no physical activity. What is happening?

The first reality that you will experience is the breath— the breath coming in and the breath going out. You are sitting quietly, and this is one activity which is going on continuously. Start observing the breath coming in and the breath going out. Just observe it. Do nothing. Don't make it a breathing exercise, by trying to regulate your breath. Don't make it *prāṇāyāma*. This exercise is totally opposite to *prāṇāyāma*. In *prāṇāyāma* you regulate your breath. That practice has its own advantages.

We are not here to condemn other techniques; they have their advantages. But as far as this technique is concerned, just observe the breath as it is. If it is deep, it is deep. If it is shallow, it is shallow. If it is passing through the left nostril, it is passing through the left nostril. If it is passing through the right nostril, it is passing through the right nostril. Just observe. Do nothing. Don't interfere with the natural flow of respiration. As it naturally comes in, you are aware. As it naturally goes out, you are aware. This is the first step to train your mind to get concentrated.

Tomorrow we will discuss the difficulites that come in this technique, and how to overcome those difficulties. We will also discuss why we use this particular technique, how it helps to purify the mind and how it differs from other techniques— how it does not work merely at the surface level of the mind, but goes to the depth of the mind. We shall try to understand all that tomorrow.

May those who have come to today's Dharma meeting get the time and the opportunity to take advantage of this wonderful ancient technique of India, and give it a trial. You will not be converted from one religion to another religion. Dharma is a pure technique of mind and matter, a science of mind and matter, the interaction of mind and matter.

How do the impurities arise, how do they multiply, and how do they overpower us? How can we stop that multiplication of the impurities? How can we eradicate them as they arise? This is what the technique will teach you. And you will not just accept it in blind faith, you will experience it yourself, step by step. It is a very scientific technique, a very rational technique, a technique which gives results here and now.

May all of you find time to take advantage of this ancient technique of our country. Come out of your misery. Enjoy real peace. Enjoy real harmony. Enjoy real happiness, real happiness.

Questions and Answers

Q: **Who is God?**

A: Truth is God. Realize the truth and you will realize God.

Q: **Please explain the difference between hypnotism and meditation.**

A: The true meditation techniques of ancient India were totally against hypnotism. Some techniques did use hypnotism, but this is totally against Dharma. Dharma makes you self-dependent. Hypnotism will never make you self-dependent. Therefore these two do not go together.

Q: **How is Vipassana different from escapism?**

A: Vipassana is to face the world. No escape is permitted in Vipassana.

Q: **Are there any liberated people living presently?**

A: Yes. It is a progressive path to liberation. As much as you are free from impurity, that much you are liberated. And there are people who have reached the stage where they are totally free from all impurities.

Q: **Which is better: temple construction, service, teaching or hospital work?**

A: All these social services are important; there is nothing wrong with them. But do them with purity of mind. If you do them with an impure mind, generating ego, it does not help you and it does not help others. Do it with purity of mind, with love, with compassion and you will find that it has started helping you, and it has started giving real benefit to others also.

Q: **We should lead a moral life, but morality is deteriorating in the whole world.**

A: It is all the more important that Dharma should arise at this time, when morality is deteriorating! The time when there is darkness all around is the time when the day should break, the sun should rise.

Q: **If a negative act is committed for the good of others, is it bad?**

A: Certainly it is bad. A negative act starts harming you. When you have harmed yourself, you can never help anybody else. A lame person can never help another lame person. First you have to make yourself healthy, and then you will find that you have started helping others.

Q: **How can we avoid bad habits like smoking cigarettes and chewing *pāna?***

A: Not only smoking cigarettes or chewing *pāna*—there are so many different types of addictions. When you practise Vipassana, you will understand that your addiction is not actually to that particular substance. It seems as if you are addicted to cigarettes, alcohol, drugs or *pāna;* but the real fact is that you are addicted to a particular sensation in the body. When you smoke a cigarette, there is a sensation in the body. When you chew *pāna,* there is a sensation in the body. When you take a drug, there is a sensation in the body. Similarly, when you are addicted to anger or passion, these are also related to body sensations. Your addiction is to the sensations. Through Vipassana you come out of that addiction. You come out of all outside addictions also. It is so natural, so scientific. Just try and you will find how it works.

Q: **Are only human beings in misery? Are other beings living a harmonious life?**

A: Misery is everywhere, but other beings can't come out of their misery because they can't observe the reality within themselves. Nature—or if you want to call it "God Almighty"—has given this wonderful power only to human beings, to observe the reality within ourselves and come out of misery. Make use of this wonderful power that is given to us.

Q: **It is against morality to kill an enemy if you are a member of the Armed Forces?**

A: Yes. But at the same time, the Army is necessary for the protection of the country, for the protection of the civilians. The Army should not be used just to kill others. It should be used to show the strength of the country, so that an enemy cannot have even the thought of being aggressive and harming people. Therefore, the Army is necessary. But not to kill, just to show strength. If somebody is harming the country, then the first thing is to give a warning. Otherwise, if it becomes necessary, action has to be taken. But then again, the soldiers have to be trained not to have anger, not to have animosity. Otherwise their minds will become unbalanced, all their decisions will go wrong. With a balanced mind, we can take good decisions, right decisions, which will be very helpful to us and helpful to others.

Q: Can a mentally retarded person gain control over himself by Vipassana?

A: It depends. If one cannot understand what is being taught, then there is no magic, no miracle in the technique. It is a mental exercise. Just as you do different physical exercises, so you do this mental exercise. One should be at least intelligent enough to understand what the exercise is, and then to practise it. There are some who have been helped, but we can't say that everyone will be helped.

Q: The Gītā says swadharma [our own Dharma] should be followed, not paradharma [the Dharma of others].

A: It depends how you interpret it. To me, *swadharma* is the Dharma of human beings. A human being has been given this wonderful faculty to observe oneself and come out of the misery, come out of the bondage. An animal cannot do this, a bird cannot do this, an insect cannot do this. If you are just living the life without using this faculty, then you are living the life of an animal, the life of a bird, the life of an insect. Then no difference between you and that being—you are not living the life of *swadharma,* you are living the life of *paradharma.* For *swadharma,* you must learn how to come out of your bondages, by observing the truth within yourself.

Q: For the last ten to twelve years I haven't been able to sleep properly.

A: Vipassana will help, depending on how properly you work. If you come to Vipassana with the sole aim of getting sound sleep, then it's better that you don't come. You should come to Vipassana to come out of the impurities of your mind. There is a disturbance because there is so much negativity in the mind, so much worry. All those worries, negativities and impurities will start getting eradicated by Vipassana, and you will start getting very sound sleep.

Q: **Is it necessary to introduce Vipassana into education?**

A: Certainly. This is an art of life, an art of living. The next generation must learn this art at a young age, so that they can live a very healthy life, a harmonious life, free from all the other things which are going on in the name of Dharma. If they understand pure Dharma, the law of nature, they will live according to the law of nature. When children are taught Vipassana in the schools and colleges, there are very good results.

Q: **If what is needed is to start practising Dharma, do we have to face adharma as an equal and opposite reaction?**

A: Yes. When you start practising Dharma, the adharma is there. The forces of adharma, the vibration of adharma— you have to fight them. But you have the strength. Ultimately, Dharma wins. If you understand what Dharma is, and if you understand how to apply Dharma within yourself, all the adharmas will get defeated—there is no doubt about that.

Q: **You always condemn ritualism, but what is wrong with expressing our respect and gratitude?**

A: There is nothing wrong with that. Respect and gratitude are not rituals. Rituals are when you don't understand what you are doing, when you are doing something just because somebody asked you to. If deep inside you understand, "I am paying respect to my parents" or "I am paying respect to a particular god or goddess"—then, see: What are the qualities of that god? What are the qualities of that goddess? Am I giving real respect to that god and goddess by developing the same qualities within myself? Am I giving real repect to my parents by developing their good qualities? If the answer is yes, then you are doing these actions with understanding, and they are not rites or rituals. But if you perform something mechanically, then it becomes a rite or ritual.

Q: **What is life after death?**

A: Every moment one is taking birth, every moment one is dying. Understand this process of life and death. This will make you very happy and you will easily understand what happens after death.

Q: **How to break adharma?**

A: Develop Dharma, and adharma will get broken.

Q: **Kindly give a few words on how students can use Vipassana.**

A: We have found good results from students who have started practising even the first part of Vipassana, concentration of mind. Their memory has become sharper, their ability to understand a subject has improved, the comprehending part of their mind has gotten better, and their nervousness has decreased. All these are very helpful to them in their studies. And along with those, character-building starts from the very beginning.

Q: **What is the difference in Dharma between Hindus and Muslims?**

A: Understand: I am not against Hindus or Muslims. I am friendly to everyone, but I am against calling them Dharma. Call them a group of people, call them a sect, but when you call that sect "Dharma," you are just deluding yourself and others. Dharma is universal. Hindu-dharma is only for a particular society or a particular sect, so it is not Dharma. It is the same with Muslim, Buddhist or Christian. They should all survive, they should have goodwill for each other. If everybody is a Dharma person, then it makes no difference whether one calls oneself a Hindu or a Muslim—they will live in a very cordial way, because they are all Dharmic people. To be a Dharma person is more important than to be a staunch Hindu or a staunch Muslim.

Q: **Are you an atheist?**

A: (Laughs.) If by "atheist" you mean one who does not believe in God, then no, I am not. I believe in God. But for me, God is not an imaginary person. For me, truth is God. The ultimate truth is ultimate God.

Q: If a person is deaf, dumb or blind from childhood, how can he live?

A: This is some bad fruits of past karma. Vipassana cannot help that. But those who practise Vipassana are taught another technique, to give vibrations of love and compassion. These are helpful to such persons.

Q: Is there a God who created the earth?

A: I have not seen such a god. If you see God, you are welcome to believe. But for me, truth is God, the law of nature is God, Dharma is God, and everything is evolving because of Dharma, because of the law. If you understand this, and live according to the law of Dharma, you live a good life. Whether you believe in God or you don't believe in God, it makes no difference.

Q: What should be the aim of life?

A: To live a good life, a healthy life—good for yourself and good for others.

Day Three:
Practising Purification of the Mind

Day Three:
Practising Purification of the Mind

Friends: we have assembled here again this evening on the bank of the Ganges of Dharma—pure Dharma, non-sectarian Dharma—to understand what pure Dharma is. Let us understand how to practise pure Dharma: how to live a life of pure Dharma, and how to get benefited by pure Dharma.

Dharma should be kept aloof from sectarian terminologies. Dharma should never be confused with Hindu-Dharma, Buddhist-Dharma, Jain-Dharma, Muslim-Dharma, Christian-Dharma, Sikh-Dharma, etc. Dharma is the universal law of nature. It is applicable to everyone, everywhere, at all times. It is the law of nature which will keep our minds free from impurities, free from negativities, free from any kind of defilement. Practising Dharma makes the mind pure—full of love, full of compassion, full of sympathetic joy, full of equanimity. A pure mind will help you to live a good life, a healthy life, a wholesome life, which is good for you, and at the same time good for others. Such a Dharmic life can be lived by anyone.

One may keep calling oneself a Hindu, a Muslim, a Buddhist, a Jain, a Sikh or a Parsi: it makes no difference. One may call oneself a Brahmin or a non-Brahmin: it makes no difference. One may call oneself a Punjabi or a Tamilian: it makes no difference. One may call oneself an Indian or a Pakistani: it makes no difference. A human being is a human being. If one understands the basic law of nature, and lives in accordance with the law of nature, without breaking this law of nature, one is bound to live a very peaceful life, harmonious life. Out of ignorance, if one breaks this law of nature, he or she is bound to become unhappy, bound to become miserable. One may call oneself by this name or that name; one may perform this rite or that ritual; one may believe in this particular philosophy or that particular philosophy: it makes no difference at all. The law is the law. Dharma is Dharma. Purity of mind is Dharma; defilement of the mind is adharma. One has to come out of adharma and live the life of Dharma.

The base of Dharma is morality, *sīla*. One should not perform any action, physical or vocal, which disturbs the peace and harmony of other beings. One should not perform any action, physical or vocal, which will hurt other beings, which will harm other beings. The base of Dharma is *sīla*, morality.

How can one practise morality? One must attain mastery over the mind. Our ancestors, the enlightened ones, gave us a very scientific technique for this. Dharma is a pure science of mind and matter, the interaction of mind and matter. Because of this interaction and because of our ignorance as to what is happening deep inside ourselves, we keep generating negativities. And we keep multiplying these negativities, which means that we keep multiplying our misery. We make ourselves unhappy and we make others unhappy.

One should understand this law of nature not merely at the intellectual level. We cannot understand the law of nature merely by listening to discourses, by listening to Dharma talks, by reading scriptures, by discussions, by intellectualization or by emotionalization. These may make us more and more confused. The only way to understand Dharma, to understand the law of nature, is to experience it. We should have direct experience of the truth, of the law of nature. We have to keep understanding the universal law with every step that we take on the path of Dharma.

Morality is the base of Dharma. At the apparent level, it appears that we are not harming other members of society when we live a moral life. So it seems that we are obliging other people, by allowing them to live a peaceful and happy life; by not harming them, by not hurting them. But at a deeper level—at the level of the law, the law of Dharma, the universal law of nature—we are actually obliging ourselves.

Those who walk on the path of Dharma should keep understanding that every time you break any *sīla,* any moral precept—any time you hurt or harm anybody at the physical or vocal level—you have started harming yourself. Actually, you harm yourself first and then you harm others, because you have to generate a tremendous amount of negativity in your mind—anger, hatred, ill will, animosity, passion, jealousy or ego, some impurity or the other—before you can perform a physical action or a vocal action which is harmful to others.

And as soon as we generate any negativity, any impurity, any defilement in the mind, nature starts punishing us. Nature does not discriminate. Nature—Dharma—is very impartial. Anybody who breaks the law is bound to be punished here and now, and anybody who lives a life of Dharma is bound to be rewarded here and now. This is the law, applicable to everyone. With this understanding, we realize that we must live a life of morality, which is good for ourselves and good for others also. Therefore we must control our minds. We must master our minds.

As we were discussing yesterday, we can train the mind to get concentrated with the help of many objects. But when we walk on the path of Dharma, scientific Dharma—where no blind faith is involved, where no imagination is involved, where no speculation is involved— we have to work with the truth, the truth as it is.

Therefore the object of concentration should be the truth as it is: the truth pertaining to oneself, the truth pertaining to your physical structure, which you keep calling "I, I, mine, mine." We have a tremendous amount of identification with this physical structure, and a tremendous amount of attachment towards this physical structure. Similarly with the truth pertaining to the mental structure, which we keep calling "I, I, mine, mine"—a tremendous amount of identification with this mental structure, and a tremendous amount of attachment towards this mental structure. One should understand what is this "I." What is this "mine"? What is this physical structure? What is this mental structure? And one should understand it at the experiential level.

The whole process of training the mind to get concentrated should simultaneously train the mind to become pure. Purification of the mind and mastery over the mind should develop side by side. Otherwise one learns only to concentrate the mind, with which one can get much power. Every concentrated mind is a very powerful mind, and it can be misused. If the base is impure, and the mind is concentrated, it is a dangerous mind. Unwholesome actions can be performed with a concentrated mind. You must have seen a crane, standing at the bank of a pond, on one leg, fully concentrated. Concentrated on what?—on looking for a fish to devour. Or a cat at a mouse hole is concentrated on waiting for a mouse to come out, so it can devour it. To be successful, your mind has to be concentrated with every action that you perform. Even one who is a pickpocket has to keep his mind concentrated to pick pockets. These are all concentrations. Someone with a double barrelled-gun is fully concentrated on the prey, ready to shoot and kill it.

These kinds of concentration are not Dharma. When the base is craving or hatred, this is not right concentration, not Dharmic concentration. The base must be free from craving, free from aversion, and always based on the truth. There should be no imagination, no speculation, no auto-suggestions, no outer suggestions, but the truth as it is.

To realize the truth, India's enlightened people of the past gave us this technique. You sit down, close your eyes, close your mouth, and do nothing at the physical or vocal level. The whole process is a process of truth-realization, a process of self-realization, the truth pertaining to yourself at the experiential level—not what the books say, not what the scriptures say, not what your guru says, not what your tradition says, not what your belief says; but the truth that you experience from moment to moment. The truth pertaining to yourself.

What is happening at this moment? There is no physical action going on, no vocal action going on. You are just observing, observing what is happening within the framework of your body. The first thing you will observe is the flow of respiration. There is a constant flow of respiration. The breath coming in and the breath going out, the breath coming in and the breath going out: you start with that. The breath is real; there is no imagination involved. The breath pertains to your own self, the reality pertaining to yourself. This reality is very gross, but it doesn't matter—truth is truth.

You have started with the truth. If you are on the Path, you will notice that every step you take will be a step on the path of truth, truth, truth. You will start with the gross truth, and you will move towards subtler, subtler, subtler truth. You will reach the subtlest truth pertaining to your physical structure, the subtlest truth pertaining to your mental structure. A time will come when it will become very easy for you to transcend the entire field of mind and matter and experience something which is indescribable, which is eternal, which does not arise, which does not pass away. It is there all the time.

This has to be experienced, and for that you have to experience the entire field of mind and matter, the field which keeps arising, passing, arising, passing. A constant process of change is taking place. This is not just to be believed; it has to be experienced. And for that experience, you start with your respiration—the breath coming in, the breath going out; natural breath, normal breath, as it comes in naturally, as it goes out naturally.

Do not use any verbalization. From my own experience, and from the experience of so many others, I know that if you start using a word along with the awareness of respiration, your mind will get concentrated very easily, very quickly, without any disturbance. In that practice, you keep repeating any word, any name, any mantra, in which you have faith, and at the same time you observe your respiration. But in this technique of truth-realization, you are not allowed to use any word, because concentration is not the aim. Concentration with purity is the aim. If mere concentration were the aim, then all these verbalizations, visualizations, imaginations, speculations and philosophizations would be helpful. You could have used them. But because this is the analytical study of your own self, the scientific study of the mind and matter within yourself, don't use any imagination, verbalization or visualization. Just be with the truth as it is.

And don't use a breathing exercise. Don't control the breath, as is done in *prāṇāyāma*. Don't control the breath. Just be aware of the breath as it comes in naturally, as it goes out naturally. If it is deep, it is deep. You are just aware that it is deep. If it is shallow, it is shallow. You are just aware that it is shallow. If it is passing through the left nostril, you are just aware that it is passing through the left nostril. If it is passing through the right nostril, you are just aware that it is passing through the right nostril. If it is passing through both nostrils, you are just aware that it is passing through both nostrils. Don't try to change the natural flow of respiration. Just observe. Mere observation, bare observation, silent observation.

In the ancient Indian language this was called *taṭastha*, which means somebody sitting at the bank of a river. The river is flowing. One who is sitting at the bank of a river has nothing to do with the flow of the river. It is just there, the natural flow of the river. This person sitting at the bank of the river is just observing, observing the natural flow. It may be fast, it may be slow. The water might be very transparent, or it might be muddy. Whatever it is, he doesn't try to change it; he doesn't make any effort.

It is an effortless observation of the truth as it is, from moment to moment, from moment to moment. This is what one has to do: observe the breath as it is. As it is, not as you would like it to be, but as it is; as it is. It is a very easy exercise. You don't have to do anything. Nature is playing its own role. The breath is just coming in naturally and going out naturally. You are just sitting at the bank of the river and observing the flow of respiration, coming in, going out, coming in, going out. What is difficult about this? It is very easy.

But if you decide to come to a ten-day course and start working with the breath, you will find it so difficult, *so* difficult. It is quite easy to understand: "Well, I just have to observe the breath, natural breath." But when you start observing it, you won't observe even a couple of breaths before the mind wanders away. Suddenly you realize: "What happened? I was here to observe my breath." And again you bring your attention back to the breath. Again you observe just one or two breaths, and again the mind has gone somewhere else. You feel very irritated: "What's wrong with me? What sort of mind do I have? It cannot even do this easy job of observing the breath!" You get annoyed with yourself.

Then your guide at the Vipassana centre will say: "Don't get annoyed. Don't generate anger. Whether you generate anger towards somebody else, or you generate anger towards yourself, it makes no difference. Just accept the reality that the mind has wandered away." You are observing the breath and your mind has wandered away. You realize: "Look, the mind has wandered away." Smilingly accept the reality. This is the reality of this moment: the mind has wandered away. All right, the breath is still there, and you start again. You start again, and again the mind wanders away. Again you realize: "Oh look, it has wandered away." Again come back to the breath. Like this, you have to work—very patiently, very patiently. It takes a day or two, then your mind starts calming down.

You were asked to observe your breath. Observing the breath, observing the breath, you have started observing your mind also: "See, this mind keeps wandering away, it keeps wandering away." You have started making an analytical study of your own mind and the truth as it is, in a very scientific way. Where has the mind wandered? To which subject has it wandered? Again it has wandered. Where? To which subject? You can't keep a diary or make notes of where it wandered, to which subject it wandered. It wandered.

But you will notice that there are only two fields where the mind keeps wandering. Either it wanders in a memory of the past, this memory or that memory, and it keeps rolling in that: "This happened," or "That happened." Or it will jump to the future—"Oh, I want this to happen in the future," or "I don't want this to happen in the future"—and it keeps rolling in the future.

As a research scholar, you will start understanding the nature of your mind. It is a slave of its own habit pattern, constantly rolling in either the past or in the future, either the past or the future. It does not want to live in the present. And you have to live in the present; you can't live in the past. The past is gone, gone forever. All the money in the world will not buy back the moment that is gone; this is impossible. You can't re-live the past; it is gone forever. You can't live in the future, unless the future becomes the present. You have to live in the present, and the behaviour pattern of the mind is that it does not want to live in the present. This is one reason why it remains agitated.

You start understanding one reason why the mind remains agitated: it does not know the art of living. With this technique of observing respiration, observing respiration, you are training your mind in the art of living, to learn how to live in the present moment. The reality of the present moment is that the breath is coming in, or the breath is going out. Be with that, as it is: live in the present. Again the mind runs away because of its old habit pattern, and again you bring it back to the present moment. You are understanding the behaviour of your mind to some extent; a beginning has been made.

Another reality that you will observe: on the second or third day, it will become clear that whether the mind wanders in the past, or it wanders in the future, there are only two types of thoughts that keep coming. They are either pleasant or unpleasant. A memory of the past may be pleasant or unpleasant. A thought of the future may be pleasant or unpleasant. You observe, "Look, a pleasant thought has arisen." Whether it is a thought of the past or a thought of the future, you will notice that one part of the mind starts rolling in this pleasant thought, and another part of the mind starts reacting to it: "Ah, wonderful. This happened in the past, and it was so good. It was wonderful, I liked it." Or: "I want this to happen because I like it, it is wonderful." There is a reaction of liking which very soon turns into craving, which very soon turns into clinging. Craving, clinging, craving, clinging.

An unpleasant thought comes—of the past or of the future —and you will notice that one part of the mind rolls in this unpleasant thought, and the other part of the mind reacts to it: "Unpleasant, no good. I don't like it, I don't like it." Aversion, hatred, aversion, hatred. Then it becomes clear that your mind is not silent for a moment: every moment there is some thought or the other, which is either pleasant or unpleasant. Whenever there is a pleasant thought, you react with craving, craving, craving. And whenever there is an unpleasant thought you react with aversion, aversion, aversion. *Rāga, dvesha, rāga, dvesha.* The mind is constantly rolling in *rāga* or in *dvesha*, in *rāga* or in *dvesha.*

Whenever you generate *rāga,* craving, you lose the balance of your mind. Whenever you generate *dvesha,* aversion, you lose the balance of your mind, you are no longer equanimous. There is no equilibrium of the mind, there is no equipoise of the mind. When you become unbalanced, you become agitated and you become miserable. So the cause of misery becomes clearer and clearer. The root of all the defilements is *rāga* and *dvesha.* And whenever you generate any defilement in the mind, every moment it is with *rāga* or *dvesha, rāga* or *dvesha.*

This is not a philosophical thought, a philosophical game, a devotional game or an emotional game; it is very scientific, very rational. You are researching how the mind works, and you are experiencing the truth about your mind. You are rolling in *rāga,* rolling in *dvesha* and becoming miserable. Then you bring your attention back to the awareness of respiration. At that moment, when the mind is with the awareness of respiration, there is no craving. You are with the present moment. You don't start craving for the breath:"I want more breath, I want more breath." The breath is there, so there is no use craving for it. When the breath is coming in, you don't have aversion towards the breath: "Go away, I don't like this breath." There is neither craving nor aversion, there is no *rāga,* there is no *dvesha.*

As you keep working for the whole day, you will start to

experience very tiny moments when your mind is really with the breath—no craving, no aversion. You are training your mind not merely to be concentrated, but also to be free from craving, free from aversion, free from impurities. This is the proper, scientific way of developing mastery over the mind. And anybody can do it, because one is working with truth. This is not a belief. The breath is there, and the breath is not Hindu, Muslim or Christian breath, Brahmin or non-Brahmin breath, Indian or American breath. The breath is the breath— natural breath, a natural phenomenon: the breath coming in and the breath going out. And the mind that is observing it is not a Hindu mind, a Muslim mind, or a Christian mind. This is how everybody's mind is working, and you are examining your own mind, how it is working.

The whole process is so scientific, so result-oriented. You get results here and now. You understand your problem, and you start coming out of your problem in a very scientific way, a very rational way. No blind faith is involved, no gurudom is involved, no exploitation is involved, no dogmatism is involved. This is the truth. This is the science of mind and matter. Great scientists of India discovered the science of mind and matter, the interaction of mind and matter.

By observing the breath, observing the breath, you will very soon reach the stage where you understand how mind and matter are interrelated. At the apparent level, the respiration appears to be merely a physical exercise, a physical activity. The breath comes in and goes out, comes in and goes out because the lungs are pumping. So does it pertain only to your physical structure? This idea is totally wrong.

When you observe it objectively, in a scientific way, it becomes so clear that your breath is also strongly related to your mind, and also very strongly related to the mental impurities. As you are observing your breath, observing your breath, some thought of the past comes and you start reacting with anger. As soon as you generate anger, you will notice that the breath has lost its normality. It is no longer normal; it becomes slightly fast, slightly hard. And once that impurity has gone away, again it becomes normal. So the breath is strongly related to your mind and strongly related to your body.

You are here to understand the nature of mind and matter, the interaction of mind and matter—the currents, crosscurrents, undercurrents that are going on within the framework of this body. You are going to examine that. That is why you have chosen the breath. And pure breath, natural breath, without any verbalization, without any visualization, without any imagination, without any kind of philosophical belief. It has nothing to do with all those. Observe the breath as breath, and this will take you further towards subtler truths.

The saints of India understood how to make a true analytical study of the truth. That is why Guru Nānak said:

> Ādi saca, jugādī saca
>
> hai bhī saca, Nānaka hosi bhi saca.

Start with the truth, and when every step is with the truth, you will reach the ultimate truth. If you start with imagination, you may get involved with a bigger imagination, under the delusion that you have experienced the truth. But you are far away from the truth. Be with the truth, however gross it may be, and you will notice that you are moving further towards the truth— subtler truth, subtler truth, subtler truth.

At this stage, a warning: having listened to this discourse, please do not start trying it on your own. It is a very delicate job—very simple, and yet very delicate. You are making a surgical operation of your own mind, moving from the surface level to the deeper, deeper, deepest level of the mind. When you make a surgical operation of the mind, deep-rooted complexes might come to the surface, and you should know how to face them. Therefore, the first time that you learn this technique, you should learn it with somebody who is experienced. Spend ten days with an experienced teacher. But after you have learned the technique in ten days, you are your own master. You have to work on it, and it is a long path. You have to walk on the Path. Nobody else will carry you on his shoulders and bring you to the final goal. You have to walk. You have to work out your own salvation. But to learn the technique, initially you must work with somebody who has experience on the Path, who has walked on the Path.

So—observing the breath, observing the breath, keeping your attention at the entrance of the nostrils, and in that area, observing the breath coming in, going out, coming in, going out—by the time you reach the third or fourth day, something will start happening there. Actually something is happening all the time, some biochemical or electromagnetic reaction is taking place on every little particle of the body, at every moment. Wherever there is life, there is a biochemical reaction, an electromagnetic reaction. But one does not know this because the mind is so gross that one cannot feel what is happening.

After practising for two or three days, one reaches the stage where one starts experiencing some sensation or the other—ordinary, physical sensations. Maybe heat, maybe perspiration, maybe throbbing, pulsing, vibrating, tingling, heaviness, numbness—something or the other is happening in that small area. Again, your guide will say, "Just observe; do nothing. Just observe. Don't react. Just observe—*taṭastha*. Observe objectively."

Nature—the truth—has started revealing itself at a subtler level. Neither like nor dislike it; just observe. And observing its nature, you will notice that it arises, and sooner or later passes away. Then something else arises, and sooner or later it passes away. It is a changing phenomenon. It keeps arising, passing away, arising, passing away. On the third or fourth or fifth day, you will reach the stage where you will feel the entire physical structure, from the top of the head to the tips of the toes, full of sensations. And in a few days' time—in some cases on the seventh or eighth or ninth day, in some cases not on the first course but on the second or third course—the entire solidity of the body gets dissolved. There is no imagination involved; this is the truth.

The great scientists of India, who were the enlightened people of our country, made an analytical study of the entire structure of mind and matter. They discovered that the body, although it appears to be very solid, is actually nothing but tiny particles, atoms. In the Indian language of twenty-five centuries ago, these tiny particles were called *kalāpas*. A *kalāpa* is the tiniest unit of the material world. The entire physical structure is nothing but a mass of tiny *kalāpas*, and they are arising, passing, arising, passing; constantly arising, passing, arising, passing. The enlightened people experienced this.

A modern scientist also says the same thing: "The entire material world is nothing but vibrations, vibrations, wavelets, wavelets. There is no solidity in the material world." He says this because he has used his apparatus, his instruments and his intellect. But the scientists of our country understood by experience. And when they understood the truth by experience, this gave wonderful results: they became enlightened. They came out of all their miseries because thay came out of all their defilements. You will understand this also as you progress further on the Path.

As you observe the realities from the gross to the subtler, subtler, subtlest level, layer upon layer of impurities will get peeled off, will get eradicted. As you reach a subtler level, you become purer. When you reach a still subtler level, you will become purer and purer. The subtlest reality of mind and matter will take you to the stage where the mind becomes totally pure. Only then can you transcend the field of mind and matter and experience something which is eternal: the truth. You can give it any name—you may call it liberation, or enlightenment, or *nirvāṇa*. These names have no meaning; you have to experience the truth yourself. And this experience of the truth is possible only when the mind becomes ultra-pure.

To make the mind ultra-pure, you have to practise this exercise of observing the truth, from the gross to the subtle, from the gross to the subtle. A stage comes when you experience the entire physical structure as nothing but a mass of vibrations. Then the reality experienced by the Buddhas, the enlightened ones, becomes very clear to you. They announced:

> Sabbo pajjalito loko,
>
> Sabbo loko pakampito, pakampito.

The entire universe is nothing but vibration, vibration, vibration: combustion and vibration, combusion and vibration. And you yourself realize this: "Yes, it is nothing but *pakampito, pakampito:* vibration. Combustion and vibration. Combustion and vibration. "

The entire universe is experienced within the framework of the body. The universe is the universe for you only when it comes into contact with your sense doors. The world of sound is the world of sound for you only when it comes to your ear sense door. For somebody who is deaf, deaf from birth, there is no world of sound. For somebody who is blind, blind from birth, there is no world of shape or colour or light. So the universe comes into contact with these five sense doors—eyes, ears, nose, tongue, body skin. Through these five sense doors, you understand that "This is the world" and "This is the universe." And when there is no contact with any of these five, because of your past experience, there is contact with the sense door of the mind. This is the sixth sense door.

A stage comes when you experience the entire physical and mental structure as vibration, vibration, vibration. If a sound has come into contact with your ear, you will notice that the sound also is vibration, vibration. The ear sense door is vibration, vibration. The sound is vibration, vibration, and as soon as it has come into contact, a new vibration has started, a new vibration throughout the body, not merely at the sense door. It is similar to when a gong is struck, and the entire gong starts vibrating. A sound has come into contact with the ear sense door, a vision has come into contact with the eye sense door, a smell has come into contact with the nose sense door, a taste has come into contact with the tongue sense door, something tangible has come into contact with the body sense door, or a thought has come into contact with the mind sense door—then there is vibration, vibration. Neutral vibration.

If you are a good Vipassana meditator, if you are a good research scholar, you will notice that as soon as a sound has come into contact with the ear, a vibration has started. Immediately a part of the mind will cognize: "Look, something has happened at the ear sense door." Or: "Something has happened at the eye sense door," or nose sense door, etc. The job of this part of the mind is to cognize that something has happened.

Immediately another part of the mind will raise its head, and ask, "What has happened? What has happened at the ear sense door? A sound has come. What sound? Oh, these are words. What kind of words? Words of praise, or words of abuse." This is the job of the second part of the mind: to recognize what has come into contact with the sense door—and not only to recognize, but also to evaluate it. "Words of abuse—very bad! Words of praise—wonderful!" This part of the mind recognizes and gives an evaluation.

And as soon as an evaluation is given, you will notice that the neutral vibration which started throughout the body starts changing. If the evaluation was given that the words are words of praise ("Ah, wonderful!"), you will notice that the vibrations throughout the body have become very pleasant. If the evaluation was given that these words are words of abuse ("Very bad"), you will notice that the vibrations are very unpleasant. Very unpleasant. The third part of the mind has started feeling the vibrations, pleasant or unpleasant.

Immediately the fourth part of the mind will raise its head, and say: "Pleasant vibrations. Ah, wonderful! I want more! This is praise. I want more, I want more!" At the apparent level it appears that what you like is the praise, but actually what you are liking is the pleasant sensations. Or it appears that you are hating the abuse: "I don't like this abuse!" Actually you are hating the vibrations, the unpleasant vibrations within you. The fourth part of the mind is the part which reacts.

It becomes so clear that it is all mind and matter: how matter is influencing the mind, and how the mind is influencing matter. How matter originates because of the mind. How the mind originates because of matter. How matter changes into mind. How mind changes into matter. The entire phenomenon becomes so clear, so clear. This is what the scientists, the great saints of India discovered. But we got involved with these organized religions, these philosophies, beliefs, dogmas, cults, rites and rituals, and forgot the real Dharma.

I was born and brought up in a very staunch Hindu family, and it is good that I was born there. I used to recite *Gītā* like most of you are probably reciting. For me it was just recitation, mere recitation without understanding what I was reciting. The meaning, the real meaning was totally lost. Without understanding it, we used to recite a verse of the *Bhagavad Gītā* in Sanskrit, which describes Vipassana:

> Utkrāmantam sthitam vā pi bhuñjānam vā guṇānvitam
>
> Vimūḍhā nānupaśyanti paśyanti jñānacakśuśa.

This describes *utkrāmantam*—the part of the mind that perceives that something or the other has happened at some sense door: *utkrāmantam. Sthitam:* the second part tries to recognize what has happened—*sthitam.* Then with this recognition, a sensation starts, pleasant or unpleasant. And *bhuñjānam, bhuñjānam*—one starts tasting it; liking it or disliking it. And *guṇānvitam, guṇānvitam*—it multiplies. This is how one starts creating more and more bondage, more and more bondage. *Vimūḍhā nānupaśyanti, paśyanti jñānacakśuśa:* one cannot practise Vipassana unless one gets the eyes of wisdom. And the eyes of wisdom will come when you practise the truth.

If you give a veneer, a colour, of some kind of belief, dogma or imagination while you are practising concentration of the mind, then you can't understand what is really happening. Just be with the truth—the truth of mind and matter and how they are interacting—and everything will become clearer and clearer.

At a higher stage, a time comes when it becomes very clear to a Vipassana meditator why one becomes miserable, and how this misery multiplies. For example, someone has abused me, and I have generated anger. If I am a good Vipassana meditator, as soon as I have generated anger, I will notice that a biochemical flow starts in the body. This biochemical flow was called *āśrava* in the ancient Indian language. Because this biochemical flow is the result of anger, it is very unpleasant. Then, because this flow is very unpleasant, I get very unpleasant sensations. And when I get very unpleasant sensations, I again react with anger. And when I react with anger, again a very unpleasant flow starts. This very unpleasant flow happens, and again I react with anger. A vicious circle has started. For hours on end, I keep rolling in anger. At the apparent level, it appears that I am generating anger because someone has abused me. But this is just the apparent truth. The actual truth is that a biochemical reaction has started within myself, and I am reacting to that biochemical flow.

The enlightened people of our country discovered the way to come out of this vicious circle. How can we come out of it? Just observe the biochemical reaction that has started. Observe the particular sensation that has started. Whenever we generate anger, passion, fear— any impurity—a biochemical reaction pertaining to that particular impurity will start in the body. And when we observe it, observe it without reacting to it, we don't multiply the reaction. As the process of multiplication stops, the reaction slowly gets eradicated, and we start coming out of it. We have not suppressed it, we have not diverted the mind to something else: we are facing the truth as it is and coming out of it, coming out of reaction.

It is so scientific, so rational, so result-oriented. It has nothing to do with Hinduism, Buddhism, Islam or Christianity. It is the law, the law of nature. No conversion is involved. One should understand this. There is a very wrong impression that by practising Vipassana one will become a Buddhist, or a Jain, or something else. Vipassana has nothing to do with that.

A few centuries ago, someone by the name of Galileo discovered that the flat looking-earth is not flat: it is round, and it rotates on its own axis. Some believed this, some didn't believe it. Gradually everybody started believing it. When you start believing this truth, you don't convert yourself to any religion. You don't become Muslim, Hindu, Christian, Jew or Buddhist.

Some time ago somebody by the name of Newton discovered that there is a law of gravity. People gradually accepted it, but they didn't become converted from one religion to another religion. Similarly, scientists, the enlightened people of India, found out how this mind and matter works: how we react; how, because of our ignorance we keep multiplying our misery by multiplying our impurity, and how we can come out of it. If we accept this, and work on it, we can come out of it.

Of course, conversion is involved, but the conversion is from misery to happiness, from bondage to liberation, from ignorance to enlightenment, not from one organized religion to another organized religion. Vipassana is a wonderful technique of our country. We should be proud of it.

It is very unfortunate that we lost this technique for two thousand years. It is very fortunate that a neighbouring country maintained it in its pristine purity, from Teacher to pupil, from Teacher to pupil, from generation to generation. Although only very few people maintained it, they did maintain it. That is why we are getting it back now. Make use of this wonderful heritage of India, the wonderful discovery of our country. Make use of it—in your own interest, and in the interest of so many others.

May these three days of Dharma talks not become just another subject of intellectual entertainment. You can go to different places to listen to discourses, to entertain your mind and to entertain your intellect. Don't make these Dharma talks an intellectual entertainment. Give this technique a trial. Work on it. Experience it. Spare ten days of your life to learn this science of India and see what is happening within yourself. See how the mind and matter react and how they keep influencing each other. See how misery arises, how it multiplies, and how it can be totally eradicated. Make use of it for your own good, for your own benefit, for your own liberation.

May all of you find time to give a trial to this wonderful technique and come out of your misery. May all of you enjoy real peace, real harmony, real happiness; real happiness, real happiness.

Questions and Answers

Q: What is the ultimate goal of life?

A: To come out of all the miseries. Because you are a human being, you have this faculty to come out of misery. Make use of this faculty.

Q: Can a non-vegetarian succeed in Vipassana?

A: When you come to a course only vegetarian food is given. But we don't say that if you take non-vegetarian food you will go to hell. It is not like that. Slowly you will come out of eating meat. You will understand for yourself the difference between the two. Your progress will certainly be better if you are vegetarian.

Q: How can we come out of inferiority or superiority complexes?

A: This is what Vipassana does. Every complex is an impurity of the mind. As that impurity comes to the surface, you observe it. You observe it, and it passes away. When you keep suppressing it, it multiplies. When you express it, you harm others. So neither express nor suppress. Just observe. Vipassana will help you to observe.

Q: Why should we work with respiration only?

A: Respiration is the truth. Respiration is related to your mind and matter, and you are here to make an analytical study of mind and matter. So you start with respiration, and then go to a deeper level of mind and matter.

Q: To live a righteous life, don't we need God's power?

A: God's power is Dharma's power. Dharma is God. Truth is God. When you are with truth, when you are with Dharma, you are with God. Develop God's power within yourself, by purifying your mind.

Q: **I am emotional, sensitive and always full of anxiety. Can these be overcome by Vipassana?**

A: Certainly. This is the purpose of Vipassana—to liberate you from all the miseries. Anxiety and worry are the biggest miseries, and they are there because of certain impurities deep within you, which will come on the surface and pass away. Of course it takes time. There is no magic involved, no miracle involved, no gurudom involved. No guru will put his hand on your head and make you a liberated person—nothing doing. Somebody will just show you the Path. You have to work out your own liberation. Walk on the Path.

Q: **Have you seen your previous birth?**

A: Every moment I am dying, every moment I am taking a new birth. This process is going on, and I keep observing it.

Q: **My professional life involves dishonesty. I cannot take up another calling as that will cause great inconvenience.**

A: Practise Vipassana and your mind will become strong. At present you are a slave of your mind, and your mind keeps forcing you to do things which you don't want to do. By the practice of Vipassana, you will get the strength to come out of this easily, and then you will find some other profession, which will be helpful to you, and which will be healthy.

Q: **How should I deal with a situation where I am abused, kicked and belittled in front of many people?**

A: In front of many or alone, what difference does it make? If somebody insults you, somebody insults you. Why react? When you start reacting, you have started harming yourself. When that person is insulting you, he wants to make you unhappy. So you say, "All right, you want to make me unhappy? Shake hands! I'll be unhappy. I'll remain unhappy. You want to make me unhappy once, but I'll continue to be unhappy for hours, or for days at a time." What is going on? What are you doing? You are harming yourself. This will become so clear by the practice of Vipassana.

Q: **What is choiceless observation?**

A: It means to do nothing. Things are just happening, and you are observing. Don't impose this belief or that belief, this dogma, that cult, this philosophy. Don't impose anything, don't create anything: let things happen naturally. Whatever is happening within you naturally is the truth, and truth is God.

Q: **What is the difference between Vipassana and concentration?**

A: Vipassana is not merely concentration. Vipassana is observation of the truth from moment to moment. You develop your faculty of awareness, your mindfulness. Things keep changing, but you remain aware: this is Vipassana. If you concentrate only on one object, which may be an imaginary object, then nothing will change. When you are with this imagination and your mind remains concentrated on it, you are not observing the truth. When you are observing the truth, it is bound to change. It keeps changing and yet you are aware of it. It keeps changing and you aware of the change. This is Vipassana.

Q: **Is meditation the only way to get liberated?**

A: Yes. Just accepting something with blind faith will not help. You have to work for your liberation. You have to find out where the bondage is, and then you have to come out of that bondage. This is Vipassana. Observe your bondage, observe your misery. Then you will find the real cause of the bondage, the real cause of misery and you will find how this cause starts getting eradicated, eradicated. Gradually you are coming out of it. So liberation comes by the practice of Vipassana.

Q: **If people practised Dharma in ancient India, why does the caste system exist today?**

A: Because they forgot Dharma. When Dharma disappears from society, then the caste system becomes strong. When there is Dharma, there can't be a caste system in society.

Q: **How to accomplish one's goals and ambitions?**

A: Purify your mind by Vipassana and you become the master of your mind. Then you will find that all the work you do at the mundane level will be successful. At the supra-mundane level also, your work will be successful. So be the master of your mind. Make your mind pure.

Q: **How many times does a person have to attend a Vipassana course?**

A: It depends, but I would say first attend for ten days, and see yourself how it has helped you. If you find that you can apply it in life, very good. Later on, go for another ten days. But the main thing is not merely going to the courses for ten days, but applying the technique in life. If Vipassana is manifesting itself in your day-to-day life, then you are practising properly. Otherwise, merely going to courses will not help.

Q: **Is there any difference between Dharma and Dhamma?**

A: There is no difference.

Q: **What do you suggest to people who cannot attend a ten-day course?**

A: Make a determination to come to a ten-day course. Without that, nothing can be done. There is no magic, no miracle. Why would I ask people to spare ten days of their life, if I could just sit here and teach them in an hour? That would be easy, but it wouldn't work. One has to spare ten days of one's life to learn the technique. It is such a deep technique, such a subtle technique, that it requires time.

Q: **Describe a typical day in your everyday life.**

A: This is what I do: I keep practising Vipassana. I keep teaching Vipassana. I make myself happy, I make others happy.

Q: **How can we remove thoughts of lust while we are studying?**

A: Not only while studying, but all the time! Lust is lust; it is harmful. Love should be pure love. Pure love is one-way traffic; you don't expect anything in return. Dharma, Vipassana, will help this lust to turn into pure love—pure love is without a trace of passion. Pure love is full of compassion.

Q: **Isn't this technique self-centred? How can we become active and help others?**

A: First you have to be self-centred, you have to help yourself. Unless you help yourself, you can't help others. A weak person cannot help another weak person. A lame person cannot help another lame person. You have to become strong yourself, and then use this strength to help others and make others strong also.

Q: After learning Vipassana, how much time daily should we spend on meditation?

A: Ultimately it will become a full-time job, and you will be aware every moment. But initially, if you practise for one hour in the morning and one hour in the evening, it will help you. It is a mental exercise. Just as you do physical exercise every day to keep your body healthy and strong, so you do this mental exercise every day to keep your mind healthy and strong.

Q: What about corruption, which is increasing day by day?

A: People have forgotten the law of nature. If these very people start observing the truth within themselves, it will become impossible for them to live a corrupt life.

Q: Can we combine two or more techniques?

A: You can combine as many techniques as you like, but don't combine them with Vipassana. Vipassana is a unique technique and combining it with anything else will not help you. It may even harm you. Keep Vipassana pure. Other techniques only give a veneer to the surface of the mind. But Vipassana makes a deep surgical operation; it takes out complexes from the depth of the mind. If you combine it with another technique, you are playing a game which may be very harmful to you.

Q: Can kuṇḍalinī be awakened by the practice of Vipassana?

A: What is *kuṇḍalinī? Kuṇḍalinī* is the activation of nerve centres on the spinal chord. By the practice of Vipassana, every atom of the body gets activated. *Kuṇḍalinī* is just a small part of that. Practise Vipassana and you will easily understand the difference between the two.

Q: Is it possible to practise Vipassana by taking guidance from a book?

A: No, never do that. That will be dangerous.

Q: **Kindly enter politics to establish Dharma in India and solve the present problems.**

A: I have read in the newspapers that politics should be kept away from Dharma. I am totally against this view. Politics must be full of Dharma. The trouble is that the country has taken Dharma to mean sectarianism. Politics must be free from sectarianism, not from Dharma. If there is Dharma in politics, it will be wonderful. The whole country will become so pure, so happy, so peaceful.

Q: **How can we become enlightened as Siddhārtha Gotama did?**

A: Everyone can become enlightened. Enlightenment is not the monopoly of Siddhārtha Gotama. He said: "Before me, so many people became enlightened, and after me also so many are going to become enlightened." Anyone who comes out of ignorance at the experiential level is an enlightened person. Any human being can practise this and become enlightened.

Vipassana Meditation centre

There are 214 Vipassana meditation centres in the world out of which 95 are in India. At all these centres 10-day, short & long residential courses are held practically every month. Out of them Dhamma Giri centre is mentioned here along with Dhamma Pattana and Global Vipassana pagoda.

The addresses of these centres, their phone nos. and Schedule of courses can be had from the following website.

Website: <www.vridhamma.org>, <www.dhamma.org>

Main Centre– Dhamma Giri: Vipassana International Academy, Igatpuri, 422403, Dist. Nashik, Tel. (02553) 244076, 244086, 244144, 244440, Website: <www.vridhamma.org>;

Email: <info@giri.dhamma.org>

Dhamma Pattana: Near Essel world, Gorai Creek, Borivali (W), Mumbai 400091; Tel: (022) 28452238, 33747501; Tel-Fax: 022-33747531, Email: <info@pattana.dhamma.org>; Website: <www.pattana.dhamma.org>

Global Vipassana Pagoda: Near Essel world, Gorai Creek, Borivali (W), Mumbai 400091;

Tel. 022-28452235

Vipassana Research Institute: Dhamma Giri, Igatpuri.

For books, CDs & Newsletter contact:

Vipassana Research Institute

Dhamma Giri, Igatpuri 422403,

Dist. Nashik, Maharashtra

Tel: [91] (02553) 244998, 244076,

244144, 244440

(Vipassana literature published in South Indian languages can be had from local Vipassana centres)

VRI publications can be purchased ONLINE also. **Please visit:**

Website: <www.vridhamma.org>;

Email: <vri_admin@vridhamma.org>

Made in the USA
Monee, IL
07 July 2026